Books by Andrew Hacker

The End of the American Era   1970
The Corporation Take-Over (editor)   1964
Congressional Districting   (1963)

The End of
the American Era

The End of
the American Era

Andrew Hacker

New York 1970 *Atheneum*

To Lois

Contents

1	The End of the American Era	3
2	Two Hundred Million Egos	9
3	Corporate America	38
4	Superfluous Americans	77
5	Civil War	96
6	An Ungovernable Nation	126
7	Ideology and Self-Indulgence	148
8	The Illusion of Individuality	158
9	Domestic Dissonance	173
10	Democracy and the Scholarly Calling	194
11	Time of Decline	209
	Acknowledgments	233
	Index	235

The End of
the American Era

1: The End of the American Era

EVERY NATION has a history.

And as a nation may trace its origins to some era in the past, so will its history suffuse the present and make a claim on its future. But these years of nationhood are always a bounded epoch: just as such an interlude has its beginnings, so must that time come eventually to its end.

Only a few decades remain to complete the era America will have known as a nation. For the United States has been embarked on its time of decline since the closing days of the Second World War.

Numerous commentators have hailed the freedoms and opportunities gained since that time, while as many others have deplored the injustice and irrationality prevailing throughout this period. Yet what has gone unnoticed is that these very tendencies can also be symptoms of a nation's deterioration and decay.

The United States is now a freer and more democratic society than at any time in its history. For by democracy I mean a temper of the mind and spirit rather than a political or economic condition. Ordinary people in this country now have a higher estimate of their endowments and broader conceptions of their entitlements than ever before. Virtually every American possesses a self-esteem hitherto reserved for a privileged or talented few. Black or white, poor or prosperous, society's successes and not a few of its failures are infected with the idea that they are equal to any or all with whom they may choose to compare themselves. If the democratic spirit may be measured by how high a valuation people place on themselves, America's claim to being a democracy should be clear and uncontested.

The extension of the democratic spirit is in largest measure the product of a continuing and accelerating technology, which in recent years has created new occupations, higher incomes, and expanded opportunities. The machines of this generation have fashioned a condition of life wherein new millions of Americans have been able to achieve self-respect and persuade themselves of their own importance. Material prosperity encourages new expectations, for as individuals advance in employment, they feel entitled to privileges never previously considered their due.

And as the nation's technology has grown more sophisticated, the more deeply have Americans been penetrated

4

by the democratic temper. The lure of higher incomes and more interesting occupations each year draws millions of citizens away from rural towns and urban neighborhoods in which they understood who they were and where they belonged. Most Americans in the past were aware that their place was at the margin of society: young people forbore to judge their elders; the poor, indigenous as well as immigrant, remained relatively subdued; and those of other than Caucasian origins were apprised of their inferior humanity.

But controls of this order can survive only when authority is acknowledged and aspirations are circumscribed. Habits of deference have been all but destroyed by the promise of greater freedom, comfort, and variation. Yet the very fact of being freed from traditional controls brings a transformation in human character; and the rapid liberation of so many Americans carries serious —and unanticipated—consequences for the society as a whole.

With the artifacts of prosperity so readily at hand, private activities become all the more enjoyable, weakening any tendency to undergo sacrifices for social ends. Whether the desideratum is material possessions or the less tangible symbols of enhanced status, the right to comforts and pleasures is conceded to all who can afford them.

If every nation has a history, so has each nation its course to run, its age of ascendancy, and its time of decline. Most experience at least one epoch of exhilarating self-confidence when the country seems embarked on a

5

mission carrying a moral for humanity. But, long or short, every such epoch must come to an end.

The United States is now about to join other nations of the world which were once prepossessing and are now little more than plots of bounded terrain. Like them, the United States will continue to be inhabited by human life; however, Americans will no longer possess that spirit which transforms a people into a citizenry and turns territory into a nation. There eventually arrives a time when a preoccupation with private concerns deflects a population from public obligations. The share of energy devoted to common concerns gradually diminishes, and a willingness to be governed is less evident.

America's terminal hour has arrived at a time when most Americans still see their nation as vigorous in potential and youthful in spirit. Few are prepared to consider the possibility that their country will never again experience the stature it has so recently known. The assumption of unending ascendancy, with its premise that man has the capacity to order his destiny, makes it all but impossible to suggest that the American interlude of nationhood will end. The very thought that America's history is no more than a finite interval has been repressed by a people persuaded of their exemption from the pitfalls which have fated other societies.

Time runs at an ever quickening tempo. If two centuries seem too brief an interval for the rise and decline of a great nation, a single generation on contemporary calendars is now the equivalent of several such epochs in the past. The era of America's nationhood has passed too rapidly for comprehension: a period of grace is usually granted wherein a society may prepare itself for difficult days to come. But even this hour of reflection has been denied in the American instance.

A nation's decline may be under way even as its power and prosperity seem at their greatest. During the very decades when the material superstructure of a people rises to new and prepossessing heights, the faults within its foundations may remain unnoticed. Moreover, social deterioration should not be seen as the product of wrong-headed policies or inadequate information. On the contrary, the erosion of controls and the rise of self-interest are historical conditions, resulting not from deliberate decisions but rather from new combinations of unanticipated circumstances.

A declining nation can continue to pursue its overseas involvements, using conscripted or mercenary manpower in efforts to carve out spheres of influence and areas of domination. Such attempts at hegemony may persist in the face of internal disruptions and despite the widening reluctance of citizens to serve and sacrifice. Thus, loss of confidence at home may be followed by a residual period during which a nation can continue exercising its might in the global arena. Power is deployed even if purpose is absent; men may be fielded even though morale is missing. The growing unpopularity of the Vietnam involvement resulted chiefly because many Americans began to sense that their nation no longer had a lesson to impart. Nevertheless, before this century is finished, the United States may find itself embarked on similar interventions—even if they, like Viet-

7

nam, are wars without will.

The very dangers and discomforts of American life result from removing controls that once limited the minds and movements of those now unsettled by current conditions. Tensions and frustrations are bound to arise when 200 million human beings demand rights and privileges never intended for popular distribution. It is too late in our history to restore order or re-establish authority: the American temperament has passed the point where self-interest can subordinate itself to citizenship. Calls for enlightened attitudes and concerted action will continue, but with little ultimate effect. Our history shaped our character, and that history will now run its course.

2: Two Hundred Million Egos

THE SPAN of a single generation has witnessed the emergence of a new American people. Lofted to new eminences by an exploding technology and stirred by the democratic spirit to new attitudes, tens of millions of quite ordinary individuals have undergone a transformation more profound than any the world has hitherto known. America is the first nation in history to have succeeded in bestowing material comfort and moral equality throughout the majority of a population. How did this happen? What will its consequences be?

Equality is primarily an attitude of mind, an outlook encouraged by widespread prosperity. The average American feels fully entitled to glance at his fellow citizens and proclaim to any or all of them, "You are no better than I am." Nor is this boast entirely a matter of wishful thinking. The vast majority of the American people have risen far above economic and psychological privation: they have experienced advances in physical comfort and palpable changes in their social condition. This accomplishment is felt by each to be a personal achievement, a due reward for persevering effort. The new American looks upon himself first, then casts his eye to those around him. The judgment he makes of himself is favorable; he can find no reason for diffidence or shame.

The postwar years are far more than a convenient textbook chapter. The generation which has come to fruition in this era differs from all of its near and distant predecessors. Indeed, what has happened in postwar America has unsettled the lives of those born in earlier decades and molded a new character for citizens of the new generation. Every American has been affected: all wear the imprint of an epoch filled with excitement, uncertainty, and the suspicion that they are part of the end of an era.

The great catalyst was the Second World War, an event marking the end of the Depression, of unemployment, of the attitudes of pessimism and despair. The war gave new lives and expectations to the American people, who began to create heightened conceptions of themselves and of their rights and role in the nation. The war was a good thing. If its manifest purpose was to defeat America's enemies, its more enduring by-product was a population with a sense of individual dignity and pride. The price America paid for this leap forward was small compared with the losses suffered by other nations and peoples: fewer than 400,000 Americans were killed. The counterbalancing gains, by any reckoning, were immense.

America's industrial plant was put back to work at full capacity: wartime needs required that production plants be rebuilt, modernized, and that executives and engineers be given free rein to utilize their organizational and technological imagination. Invulnerable to the raids of enemy aircraft, our productive capacities were expanded and improved. The war's end saw a gigantic complex of assembly lines and offices, warehouses and distribution facilities, all primed to serve the postwar society. Indeed, plans for this transition were made even while the war was in progress. Time, personnel, even materials could be spared to prepare for peace. The American economy was never placed on a full wartime footing, and all memories of "shortages" must be viewed in perspective. There was enough to go around for both civilians and the military, for guns and for butter.

Almost fifteen million young men entered the armed services and the great majority found there a better life than they had known as civilians. They ate better, were better clothed, and enjoyed more amenities. If anything, our military establishment was too abundantly provided for: certainly the food, equipment, and accommodations furnished them were far beyond what is necessary to keep a soldier alive and moving. Other nations fielded armies supported by a fraction of our wherewithal and those men fought as well as ours, if not better. But our forces did not consist simply of soldiers: they were

American soldiers, and hence required three-course meals, recreational facilities, comfortable changes of clothing, and more than token pay.

Most of our soldiers, furthermore, were not fulltime warriors. The majority staffed, serviced, supplied, and generally served as coordinating clerks of a military organization. Some did work that was challenging and others did not. But on the whole the war years were, for those in uniform, the best years they had thus far experienced. And it was inevitable that they would want similar comforts once hostilities were terminated. Even those who had had jobs throughout the Depression remembered that it had been a tense, uneasy, and anxious time. The war years, on balance, were happier and more satisfying.

Civilian America also had a good war. Meat was rationed, but families nonetheless had more of it served on their tables than they had had during the 1930's.* Apart from automobiles, virtually everything continued to be produced in abundance: clothing, movies, magazines, candy—indeed, it is difficult to think of more than a handful of commodities that were not available to civilians. (If evidence for this is needed, examine the wartime issues of any newspaper to see the impressive array of goods and services advertised for sale.) The national balance sheet showed that a substantial proportion of our economic output went for war production, but two countervailing facts should not be forgotten: on the one

* During the three-year wartime period, 1942 through 1944, *civilian* consumption of meat was 441 pounds per capita. During the last three years of the Depression, 1937 through 1939, per capita consumption had been 376 pounds.

hand, much of the nation's "war production" actually went to provide a high standard of living for that sizable portion of the population connected with the military effort; on the other hand, the weight of goods allowed for home use compared favorably with what civilians had consumed during the 1930's. The endemic wartime complaints about "shortages" arose from frustration of expectations only recently established.

War industries with their cost-plus contracts paid well, and other employers were compelled to match those scales if only to retain their staffs. There were jobs for all who wanted them, and the fact that people were eagerly sought by a previously hostile job market instilled in them the idea that they were no longer superfluous human beings. The "Black Revolution" of our time can trace its origins back to 1942 when black Americans discovered that Help Wanted advertisements were also addressed to them. The revolution in the family had its beginnings when women went off to work, discovering that life could be varied, interesting, and independent. And the revolution in the nation's topography started as people poured forth from small towns and the countryside to take up the jobs being proffered in the metropolitan areas. By the same token, the movement westward mounted at an accelerated pace as the new life of California ceased being a Hollywood dream and became an attainable reality. Once started, the momentum of these beginnings would never be undone. If the circumstances of war convince a person that he is no longer the manner of being he has previously been, and if events combine to persuade him that he can become the creature he has always wanted to be, then he will not willingly revert to his former self simply because peace has been declared. There would be no returning to the farm and the small town; there would be no exodus from the major metropolitan areas; there would be no backward movement from the West Coast to the Eastern Seaboard. Nor would the nation's blacks—or its women—voluntarily revert to submissiveness and subordination.

The war also hastened the slow process of ethnic assimilation. Many of the combatants may have borne names of recent European arrivals, but once garbed in their country's uniform they became full Americans. (In an all-too-familiar scene, the sergeant called the recruit-camp roll: "Kowalski, O'Brien, Goldstein, D'Amato, Brown.") The melting pot had been fusing since 1924, when the last significant numbers of immigrants from Southern and Eastern Europe gained admission to our shores. But the economics of the Depression and the psychology of prejudice had kept Irish, Italians, Poles, and Jews submerged in their ethnic ghettoes. The stories about Stupid Swedes, Avaricious Jews, Criminal Italians, and Drunken Irishmen were publicly told with little regard for the sensibilities of those affected. However, the war saw the end not only of ethnic humor but of many of the characteristics which once gave credence to the jokes. People who in 1941 were regarded as Kikes or Micks or Wops had by 1946 become simply Americans. That half-decade did a work of assimilation that would otherwise have taken at least two generations.

Accompanying the breakdown of ethnic barriers was the upsurge in geographic movement. Not only were those in the services transferred to distant parts of the country, but a good proportion of the civilian labor force voluntarily moved to new jobs in new locations. These shifts marked the beginning of the transformation of the urban ghetto, and signaled the destruction of the close-knit enclaves that had been the chief reinforcement of European ethnic identities.

Thus the war implanted in second- and third-generation offspring of immigrants an impatience to accelerate their assimilation into the mainstream of American life. Whereas resignation and despair had been the hallmarks of the Depression, the war had the effect not only of raising hopes but of creating opportunities and incentives as well. A man might continue to bear an Italian name, but if he dressed and spoke and behaved like an unhyphenated American, he stood a good chance of being accepted into the institutions symbolizing success and status. Corporations and universities had been cool to the applications of virtually all but Anglo-Saxons, but the army was willing to grant commissions to any man with brains and ambition. Thus the Kowalskis and the D'Amatos who became lieutenants began to raise new postwar vistas for themselves. But they also understood that to achieve these prominences they would have to abandon the external attributes of their ethnic heritage.* Indeed, the need had passed to change one's name or religion, as the new arrivals learned how to make themselves all but indistinguish-

---

* Except for the few who would enter politics. It is revealing to notice how, say, a third-generation Irish-American who aspires to political success will continue to stress his "Irishness." Had he chosen a corporation career, he would eschew manners or mannerisms that might call attention to his ethnic background.

able from the third- and fourth-generation Americans who sat beside them in the office or lived next door on the suburban tract.

While the majority of returning servicemen did not take advantage of the G.I. Bill's benefits, a large proportion of those who did were people who would not otherwise have gone to college. Institutions of higher learning —especially state universities—generously opened their doors to a wave of postwar applicants, many of whom were not socially or academically "qualified" by prewar standards. These Americans, upon graduation four years later, looked forward to entering a new stratum of society: they took for granted that positions befitting their status and education would be waiting for them. In this they were not disappointed.

During the Second World War the American economy had learned some significant lessons in efficiency. The improvements in productivity that were achieved did not, as classical economic theory might have dictated, bring about a reduction in the prices of commodities and services. Even if it took fewer man-hours to manufacture a car or a bar of soap, the cost to the consumer remained the same. Thus postwar business found itself taking in a good deal of unanticipated money—far more than was needed for paying dividends to stockholders and too large an amount to be consumed even by replacing old machinery or building new facilities. To be sure, no business organization regarded this windfall income as superfluous cash. It was seen rather as money that could be liberally expended on hiring new employees.

Were all these new job-holders really needed? This is

a question best not asked, for an objective answer is impossible. Of course certain functions must be performed if goods are to be manufactured, distributed, and eventually sold. However, it is never clear just how many hands —or minds—are needed to carry out this elaborate process. Nevertheless, anyone having supervisory responsibility for the completion of a task will invariably protest that his staff is too small for the assignment at hand. During the postwar period, demands for added employees have been accommodated as never before. Millions of new jobs were created and salaries provided, and staffs expanded even where it could not be proved that the presence of such new bodies would in time pay for themselves in increased earnings. This postwar white-collar explosion occurred because new technology made new financial resources available. Most white-collar jobs come into being not so much because they are needed (that can never be proved) but as and when the cash can be found to underwrite them. And it was into these openings that millions of young veterans poured. They donned white shirts, sat down at desks, and went to work.

Just what does "work" consist of for these Americans? How do they "earn" their salaries? Questions of this sort can be answered only in the vaguest of terms, for hours spent talking with people and poring over paper are all but impossible to relate to tangible results. Still, there is emerging a vocabulary purporting to explain how the white-collar day is consumed: such individuals are paid to manage and plan and coordinate; they travel and confer and investigate possibilities; they sit at meetings and talk on the telephone; they write letters and draft memoranda; they check up to see how things are coming along; they accompany their superiors and provide additional opinions; they relate to suppliers and retailers, stockholders and unions, government agencies and the public. With all these tasks to be accomplished, their salaried time is easily filled, spreading over into prolonged lunch hours and often into dinner and the evening.*

This new white-collar class, now of great proportions in the nation's economy, ranges from hundreds of thousands of clerks to a handful of top executives. Its members are distinguished by the fact that they do not get their hands dirty and have dissociated themselves from those who do. They are sincerely persuaded that they are earning their incomes, and they are convinced that the functions they perform are absolutely essential for the survival of the organizations with which they are affiliated.

There may be—and probably are—too many construction workers on a building site. There is no apparent need for a fireman in a Diesel cab or a flight engineer in a jet cockpit. Such superfluous employment is generally agreed to be "featherbedding." But postwar folklore insists that there can be no such thing as "white-collar featherbedding" in the offices and anterooms of the glass-and-aluminum buildings flanking New York's Park Avenue or Chicago's Loop or rising in San Francisco or

---

* No longer is it possible to tell how important an individual is from the description he gives of his job. White-collar titles are grander than ever before and give little hint of the responsibilities they may or may not involve. This is especially the case with new "staff" and "professional" positions, where the jobholder does not supervise a department composed of people who can be counted. The only index left of a person's prominence is his salary, and that, of course, is a tightly held secret.

18

Houston or Denver. Indeed, the common view is that those who toil in these air-conditioned purlieus are already overworked. Hence, of course, the continual construction of even more of these towers: to provide more desk space for the fresh reinforcements to the white-collar workers of corporate America.*

According to the traditional logic of business, increased earnings due to advances in productivity are applied toward reductions in prices or—more likely—higher profits for the owners. Fortunately for postwar America, this antediluvian logic is no longer implemented. Had it persisted, modern managements would make as cold a scrutiny of each new request for an additional white-collar position as it customarily does for adding extra blue-collar employees. And had such tests been imposed, there would have emerged the realization that most of the new white-collared planners and coordinators, deputies and associates, assistants and assistants' assistants, were never needed at all. The economic contribution of these desk-occupiers would in all too many cases be found to be nil or even negative.

The old economic logic was made for an era of scarcity when cash had to be portioned according to stringent priorities. That logic also accompanied austerity in the

---

* By "corporate" I mean not simply large businesses but also non-profit organizations which are similar in structure. If the corporation stands at the eye of the economic whirlwind, alongside it have been foundations and universities, churches and trade associations, medical centers and quasi-governmental agencies. These, too, have been accumulating the cash with which to pyramid their staffs and thus provide an expanding sector of employment. Moreover, every grant made by a foundation or a public authority spawns a project or an institute or an agency which, in turn, creates even more white-collar jobs.

office, for often the manager was the owner and wanted all of the surplus to take home for himself. Hence he could get along with a rolltop desk for himself in a room shared with an ancient bookkeeper and a maiden secretary. (If he had a private railroad car or a yacht, it was for his private enjoyment. He might pay $100,000 of his own money for those luxuries, but he would still keep the bookkeeper's salary at $10 a week.) It was, too, a day when taxes were so low that a dollar in profits was worth 95 cents. However, it will not do to attribute today's white-collar explosion to high rates of taxation. Even if the government takes 50 cents out of every profit dollar, the remaining 50 cents is still 50 cents. Hiring a new employee at $10,000 salary may "cost" the organization only $5,000; but $5,000, when multiplied by several thousand such positions, is a serious amount of money for any balance sheet.

What really defeated the old logic was the rise of a new managerial temperament. The new supervisor is an employee, a salaried executive rather than an entrepreneur. He is of course concerned with profits; but he seeks to optimize rather than maximize those earnings: that is, his organization need earn only enough to pay a conventional dividend, with an appropriate amount remaining for depreciation and investment. A large firm can achieve this quite easily and still have left over the wherewithal to augment its white-collar echelons.*

* Of course a business can never relax: orders do not come in automatically, and the bids of competitors must be met or matched. However, keeping one's relative position in an industry is not that difficult. At any rate, a corporation should no more be congratulated for remaining solvent and making a profit than any individual should be

Also encouraging the expansion of white-collar employment have been its attendant social and psychological pleasures. For more and more individuals, the significant creature comforts of life are enjoyed at the place of work as much as at home. The modern office, with its spacious amenities, provides as pleasing a setting as any suburban home or town apartment. Business meals are usually superior to home-cooked fare, business travel is relaxing if not adventurous, and conferences at work are far more stimulating than their domestic counterparts. Moreover, the social climate on the job is convivial, leisurely, and plainly provides the best part of the breadwinner's day. Such conviviality is possible because employers are willing to provide a more-than-ample supply of people for this purpose. If office staffs were pared down to those hands and minds which were actually essential, there would be no time for friendly coming-and-going that now consumes so much of the day. And if about half of each white-collar working day is occupied with nonproductive activity, then twice as large a staff is required to get any job done.

Certainly the inflation of white-collar occupations is now necessary for the prosperity of the economy. Millions of Americans continue to pour out of the nation's high schools and colleges, and many others are graduating from declining expiring blue-collar jobs. These people need honorable employment, and little good can come from too rational a scrutiny of a development

given a medal for keeping a job and bringing home a weekly check. All participation in the nation's economy, whether by corporations or individuals, is competitive.

which has kept much of the population interestingly occupied and pleasantly provided for.

The new American is best characterized as someone who has left home and no longer has the need or desire to return to the setting in which he was raised. For millions of Americans who spent their youth on farms, in small towns, or on the streets of large cities, those ties were severed by entering military service, by going away to college, or by taking a first job in a faraway city. Although the patterns of migration vary—from New England to New York City, from the Deep South to Southern California, from the Middle West to Houston or Phoenix or Florida—the particular route followed is less crucial than the time of occurrence. Most make the break at the start of adulthood.

These migrations are not due to any "restlessness" inherent in the American spirit. Most people would probably prefer to stay where they are, and a majority would certainly like to settle down after one transplantation. The largest number move for economic and occupational reasons. The lure of superior earnings and the prospect of more enjoyable occupations cause individuals to change their homes and recast their personalities. In this way technology reshapes societies and transforms the history of nations.

Two related factors accelerate the economic component. The first is that childhood settings are too stifling. City slums and small towns are essentially inequalitarian, and the typical resident is not unaware of his powerlessness in these circumstances. For all the references to the

yeoman democracy of rural areas, with textbook eupho-
ria over town meetings and broad-based participation,
the fact remains that a small commercial and professional
class usually dominates the politics and economy of such
regions. Opportunities to succeed are few, for the local
gentry of provincial America is virtually impenetrable.
The pattern of urban power is rather different, for here
class rule has long since expired. Nevertheless, those who
occupy lower-class neighborhoods see themselves faced
with a "system"—part political, part bureaucratic, part
economic—which leaves few opportunities for personal
advancement. In these interstices of an older America it
is difficult, if not impossible, for an average person to at-
tain fulfillment.

And this, of course, is what is now wanted. Americans
expect—indeed, feel entitled to—the best that life has to
offer. They aspire to live lives of the sort that others they
deem no different from themselves have been able to secure. This ambition is the chief lubricant of accelerated
movement. It is not uniquely American and is certainly
not new in our time. Still, compared with other nations,
America has had fewer people willing to content themselves with the existence assigned to them by birth and
upbringing.

Yet a price is paid by one who abandons his past. The
characteristic points of departure and arrival in the postwar trek have been the settled community and the always unassimilated suburb. The former may have been a
churchbound village or a boisterous city slum, but residence there imparted a knowledge of who one was and
where one belonged. The suburban stopping-places of

mobile Americans are too new, too heterogeneous, and too lacking in fixed institutions to give either an identity or a meaningful role to their residents. Thus the fact of movement is much more than simply a physical separation. For adjustment to so different an environment requires the creation of a new personality and the adoption of new values.

The American who makes the break from his home soon discovers that he cannot carry his old values with him and at the same time effect a successful assimilation for himself. He can still believe in God, but the fundamentalism of his earlier creed will have to be exchanged for worship in more sophisticated and less authoritarian accents. He may even alter his table habits, abandoning provender once familiar but no longer fashionable. He will probably see less and less of the parents he left behind, regarding them not without affection but as citizens of another country no less than another generation.

More and more marriages are some form of intermarriage. Even ignoring the more exotic varieties of mixed matings—between Christians and Jews, between Catholics and Protestants—new alliances being contracted have less and less of an ethnic or sectarian overlay to them. The wedding of a Baptist and a Presbyterian foretells a bland Protestant future with little loyalty to old creeds and churches. The marriage of a Polish and an Irish Roman Catholic similarly produces children unaffiliated to an earlier generation by ties of nationality. Not only does religion lose much of its traditional and doctrinal underpinning, but personal identity is weakened and compensatory substitutes for old ties are not easily devised.

The most common challenge revolves around the creation of new values. This is not so difficult a task as might first be thought once it is understood that new modes of comportment involve style rather than substance. By now the rules of adaptation are well known: one should be personable and display an interest in others; be positive and constructive; adjust and join in. If adjustment is the key, what is noteworthy is that so many have carried it off so well. In large measure they have been able to accomplish this feat because each is surrounded by others who are in much the same position. All are newcomers and everyone is cautious for fear of making a wrong move. All are aware of one another's vulnerability, and no one is an alien in a land where everyone is a stranger.

Patterns of adjustment are best seen in the confrontation of new situations: in raising children, in accumulating material possessions, in the uses of leisure. Yet few individuals are made of such stern stuff that they can repudiate the strictures by which they were guided in their formative years. Thus the vocabulary of piety and character, of individualism and achievement, lingers even though contradicted by the behavior of those who continue to intone those sentiments.

The new American is not oblivious to the fact that he has been backsliding. There are moments when he doubts the virtue of continual adjustment. He knows, for example, that he is not able to command the respect of his children as his parents commanded his. It is not inconceivable for him to be a figure of authority to his offspring, but to accomplish this would require an uncomfortable measure of self-discipline and would in-

25

crease the risk of being considered old-fashioned. While it is theoretically possible to be firm in preventing one's children's behavior from being shaped by their youthful peers, the mass media, and other permissive influences, the very establishing of parental authority can undermine the image one has painstakingly developed in order to achieve success in his community and career. He will frequently experience moments of misgiving, accompanied by sensations of betrayal and feelings of guilt. Few can admit to themselves that they are blameworthy for their own transgressions, and the usual alternative is to focus on the lack of character and self-discipline in others. Far better, indeed, to reserve one's comments for those who may be readily identified as lesser breeds in society by the weaknesses seen as typical of their status or origins.

The continuing influence of puritanism should never be underestimated. The puritan catechism, with its emphasis on the deferral of gratifications and the avoidance of indulgence, formed the childhood lessons of most modern adults. The difficulty is that the puritan ethic was made for an era of scarcity. Temptation could be avoided if it was seldom available. But affluence encourages promiscuity: not only in sex, but in the accumulation of all the amenities which comfort the body and stimulate the senses. If an individual's behavior violates the imperatives of his early instruction, self-hatred is engendered which is bound to have consequences. The customary outlet is rationalization: hence efforts at persuading yourself that you have earned (and therefore deserve) life's pleasures; indeed, that you are too strong to be corrupted by enjoying your existence. In this dialectic what remains is the puritan assumption that, for all your sybaritism, you are still a unique and superior person. Rising out of this conviction is the search for indulgence on the part of one's putative inferiors who have yet to earn their enjoyments.

For all this, the new American is informed, educated, and possessed of far greater sophistication than any nation's ordinary citizen has ever before been. He is more fully aware of how his society functions and of his relative place in it. Through his exposure to a variety of media and his own widening experience, he is not unacquainted with the outlines of politics, history, and even a smattering of sociology. The new American even realizes that he is himself an object of study, and a certain self-satisfaction emerges as he reads and hears that he is both typical and normal. The contemporary citizen can no longer be shocked by new approaches to sex or religion or politics: he has heard everything even if, at times, he does not like what he hears. It is difficult to imagine a fact, an idea, a proposal that has not been heard before or which is any longer capable of arousing astonishment or indignation. This is the final evidence of how completely Americans have adjusted: they are prepared to adapt themselves to change, no matter what the substance of that transition may be.

The whole issue of "class" in American life is a vexed one, and no attempt will be made here to unravel the intricacies of research and speculation in this area. America clearly is not a "classless" society, for the persistence of relatively impermeable lines of striation prevents a large proportion of Americans from bettering their condition of life.

I will argue here that there are only two significant classes in the United States today. To be sure, any student of sociology can locate a half-dozen or more strata among 200 million Americans, determined by income distribution or occupational and educational attainment. However, for my purposes a more simple-minded approach is in order. I will distinguish between those who have achieved relative success in the recent generation and those who have been left out or behind. The former class now constitutes the American majority: productive citizens who have attained respectable incomes and an honorable position in the social scheme of things. The latter class is now a minority: superfluous people without steady employment or means of support, and looked upon with no small fear and disdain by those who have attained superior status.

I prefer to speak of all—or virtually all—successful Americans as "middle-class." But if I do so, it is with full realization that there are obvious distinctions within their ranks, most particularly between individuals who do relatively dirty work for hourly wages and those who are paid weekly or annual salaries to deal with paper and people. Yet even here the differences may be matters of style more than of substance. An increasing portion of working-class Americans are securely employed, well paid, own their own homes, and send their offspring to college. While working-class manners and morals differ from middle-class standards in many major particulars, the more consequential point is that even blue-collar workers now regard themselves as successful by postwar American standards. At the same time, as will be indicated, most people who work at white-collar jobs share many essential attributes with individuals having less sanitary occupations. Therefore, if my comments focus on Americans who earn their livings in or around offices, this is simply because they now comprise the greater part of the nation's labor force and dominate the postwar population. I will—as have others—refer to this group as the "new middle class."

Not all Americans belong to the new middle class, nor can the possibility be held out that everyone will in time be recruited to it. At this point, however, a majority of the economy's productive citizens hold its attitudes, either in objective fact or subjective outlook. These Americans have made it and are with it, and have managed to ally themselves to the technological underpinning and organized institutions of the epoch. And because this class of Americans is new, its membership deserves scrutiny and discussion. While it has features in common with middle classes the world has known in the past, it is distinguishable from its predecessors in significant ways.

The contemporary middle class is, first of all, large. It encompasses the bulk of the employed population, ranging from schoolteachers and sales clerks to lawyers and presidents of corporations. Everyone who receives a regular weekly or annual salary and deals with people and paper rather than the actual processes of manufacturing is middle class both in fact and in title. While niceties of distinction can be made between the "lower" and "upper" divisions of this class, what is important to note here is that the middle class extends into the highest reaches of the society. For America has only an infinitesimal upper class consisting of individuals of old family and inherited wealth. Even business and professional men earning $100,000 a year are still basically middle class, not only in outlook but also because they are transitory occupants of positions rather than generators of fortunes or dynasties.

The large—and unwieldy—size of this class at once distinguishes it from the middle stratum of earlier generations. Until recently the middle class of any country was always surprisingly small, relative to the total population. Consisting of self-employed businessmen, professional people, and the more prosperous farmers, it encompassed not more than 10 or at most 15 percent of the nation.

The question of relative size requires emphasis if only because the values and behavior associated with middle-class life were developed to fit a stratum to which few were permitted entry. Those standards of comportment could be exacting because they were applied only to a limited group. Many of the quandaries arising in recent years stem from the fact that conventional middle-class standards are now expected from the greater part of the population. Not surprisingly, the new middle class has shown itself unwilling and unable to adhere to rules tailored for a quite different group of individuals in quite different settings. While certain canons of deportment can reasonably be expected of 10 or 15 percent of a population, it is unrealistic to assume that the same behavior can be effectively induced in a group approaching two-thirds of a citizenry. In short, the American middle class, by its numerical inflation, has bestowed white collars and heightened expectations on people who in an earlier age would have had quite different stations in, and outlooks toward, life.

Ascension to middle-class incomes and occupations is always accompanied by a new conviction of a superior status. Thus more Americans now feel entitled to privileges and amenities which were once reserved for only a few. Members of the new middle class, for example, demand to be protected from crime and violence. They are upset when taxis are unavailable, when planes fall behind schedule, and when roads and recreational facilities are overcrowded. They object to the quality of service they receive from others and the lack of people prepared to wait on them in return for a reasonable payment. These are traditional middle-class anticipations. But when six out of every ten people harbor such expectations, it is time to inquire why so many feel entitled to special status and preferential treatment.

The fact is that the egos of 200 million Americans have expanded to dimensions never before considered appropriate for ordinary citizens. More aggravating than the crowding that comes with sheer growth of population is the exacerbated sensation of congestion arising when the individuals who rub against each other have heightened evaluations of their own merit and keener sensitivity to such abrasions. Most Americans now feel that they should be guaranteed physical safety, a sufficiency of elbow room, and protection from psychic jostling. Any

31

discussion of crowding must take account not only of bodily proximity but also of the self-estimate of those who comprise the multitude. Indeed, most of the feelings of exasperation about contemporary American life come from the fact that many more people now feel deserving of protections and privileges once accorded to only a few.

A related feature of the new middle class is that it is national in character. The middle classes of earlier times were primarily local, consisting chiefly of the *burghers* of a city or county—merchants, professional men, factory owners, and well-to-do farmers. What such individuals had in common was status and power in their community, and out of this condition grew the structure of the nation's politics and the vitality of regional interests and ethnic variations.* These patterns, however, are fast dissolving.

As has been indicated already, one attribute of the new middle class is its transiency. These newly arrived Americans are prepared to sever their old attachments and

* The entire political system—especially in its party organization and legislative branches—evolved as institutions controlled by local middle classes. The personnel of party committees and delegations is still predominantly self-employed businessmen and professional men of long residence in one place, and legislative representatives continue to give sympathy and sustenance to the interests of local enterprises. Thus, a large part of the nation's political mechanism is even now geared toward an earlier America, passing laws and producing candidates generally oblivious to the needs of a national society. These individuals and institutions are not only well entrenched, but the basic rules by which the political game is played have long been stacked in their favor. Intrusion by outsiders is extremely difficult and reform is almost impossible. Any restructuring to render the parties and legislatures less parochial will have to find a counterweight powerful enough to dislodge the local middle class. Certainly the new middle class is not the most apt candidate for such an undertaking.

move to new locations with an alacrity that surpasses the legends of pioneer days. Almost gypsy-like in their willingness to pursue new careers in whatever part of the country their employer or their search for employment sends them, they become truly national in their outlook. A man who once claimed Flatbush or Fayetteville as his home now regards the whole country as his residence. The question thus arises: Is it *possible* to be a citizen of a huge nation in any but the most nominal sense? For the concept of citizenship—particularly for the middle class —always had its definition in the context of a discrete and identifiable locale.

The great philosophers of citizenship—Plato, Rousseau, Jefferson—insisted that only in the setting of a small community could civic and political participation have substantial meaning. The relation of person to person, and hence of authority to the individual, had to be intimate and based on direct understanding. However, the bonds tying Americans to local loyalties have been severed and viable substitutes have not been developed to take their place. Certainly there is no sense of national loyalty to replace the local affections, nor is there any great sign that compensatory ties have emerged in the lives of most Americans. As a result, the new middle class plays less of the citizen role than did its more solidly entrenched predecessor.

Indeed, American "pluralism," essentially a characterization of the old middle class, becomes an increasingly superficial description of the postwar society. Does it actually matter that we can be Methodists or Lutherans, that we hail from Ohio or Oregon, that our grandparents were Germans or Swedes? These plural features may add color to the national landscape, but their influence on attitudes and behavior is more apparent than real at a time when much of America is becoming a single homogeneous nation.

At this point it is probably worth asking whether these nationalizing and homogenizing processes are transforming America into a "mass society." The phrase, unfortunately, carries many ambiguous meanings. Certainly more Americans now have more in common with one another than did their parents, and uniformity in taste is doubtless growing. I would also agree that group loyalties—to churches, trade unions, and kindred community associations—tend to be paper memberships rather than deep personal involvements. Individuals are indeed very much alone and on their own. (Whether they are thereby "alienated" or deprived of an "identity" is another matter.) In addition, much of the economic and organizational power in American society is concentrated in large institutions which can make far-reaching decisions without having to account to any readily identifiable constituency. If all these are the ingredients of a "mass society," then that is what America now is or is fast becoming.

Yet at the same time I am suggesting that the nation is fundamentally democratic because it has liberated its citizens from hitherto prevailing controls, enabling them to create new and heightened estimates of their qualities and capacities. Whether or not these people have power really depends on the issues involved. My own view is that majority rule frequently prevails, but not usually through elections or by conscious design. The majority exercises its power by creating an atmosphere which makes life uncomfortable for those who disregard accepted precepts of conduct, and it enforces these sanctions not only on deviant outsiders but also over its own members.

Perhaps most critical of all is the fact that members of the new middle class are not people of property.* The rationale for private ownership of property is as valid today as it was two and three centuries ago when adumbrated by Adam Smith and John Locke. A man's property is a hedge, inasmuch as it provides an identifiable area of freedom for its owner. Within those boundaries an individual is free to do as he pleases: to express his personality, develop his capacities, and be as creative as his talents allow. And—to change metaphors—property is also a pedestal: it gives its owner an extension to his personality, affords him a more imposing plateau on which to stand. Thus men of property have always had authority and security denied to those without it: the ownership of property, to paraphrase, makes some men more equal than others. For these reasons the hope is held out that independence of mind and freedom of action may be expected from individuals having a secure income. Indeed, the great—and often hazardous—advances in civil liberties and constitutionalism were almost invariably led by the propertied middle classes. If Thomas Jefferson called for a nation where all would be property-

---

* Let me make clear that I do not consider ownership of a car, a home, or even a modest portfolio of stocks to be property. Property, by any meaningful measure, is the possession of wealth-producing instruments which yield a secure and substantial income for the owner.

owners, it was because he realized that men in a condition of economic dependency are less apt to take controversial stands or make public their views on divisive questions.

The smaller middle classes of earlier generations were propertied classes, and their self-disciplined individualism was created by and for this secure and independent stratum. Any expectation that an essentially propertyless class will adhere to such rules of behavior is surely futile. For postwar America's new middle class stands in a continual condition of dependency. Its members are employees, and their livelihoods are always contingent on the approval and good will of the individuals and organizations who employ them. Such a class will inevitably be cautious, uncontroversial, and attuned to the sensibilities of those around them. Looming over every such person is a perpetual atmosphere of insecurity: not so much the fear of losing his job at the end of the week as the understanding that through all of his life he will be in a dependent position. Whatever status and prosperity today's middle-class American may have is due to the decision of someone to hire him and utilize his services. He knows that there is virtually no chance of escape from a system compelling him to meet standards set by others.

No real point is served by attempts to alter conventional terminology. To call the contemporary middle class by some other name can only cause needless confusion. What needs emphasis is that this group lacks the significant characteristics of past middle classes in American society. It is expansive rather than attenuated, national rather than local, and propertyless and dependent rather than propertied and secure. In fact, the new middle class has many attributes in common with the traditional conception of a proletariat. And it is possible to argue that those who were once known as the working class have simply put on white collars.

An enhanced standard of living and the accumulation of material comforts have not altered the basic character of the American people. Once this is acknowledged, much of the behavior of postwar Americans comes into focus. The new majority may be conservative, self-centered, and lacking class-consciousness in the Marxian sense—but then it was Marx's lament that so few workers were aware of their true class position and interests. If they think of themselves as middle class and expect the accouterments of their newly achieved status, they are nevertheless quite ordinary people of average intelligence and commonplace talents. These new Americans constitute a new presence in many important ways, but, from a significant standpoint, their rightful forebears are not the old middle class but rather the peasants and proletarians of an earlier time.

3: Corporate America

SINCE THE END of the Second World War the corporate form has emerged as the characteristic institution of American society. Its rise has made time-honored theories of politics and economics irrelevant, and its explosive growth has created new breeds of men whose behavior can no longer be accounted for by traditional rules of conduct.

America is not yet dominated by the corporate way of life, but the corporation is central to the nation's economy. The 150 largest firms produce more than half of our country's manufactured goods, and the 500 largest own over two thirds of the productive assets of the nation.

There remains, of course, a substantial part of the economy which cannot be called corporate. The small-business community still embraces most of the working and entrepreneurial population. Yet all signs indicate that the future lies with the great corporate institution, and no one seriously contends that there will be a rebirth of small business or a reduction of corporate growth. If not presently typical of our economic or social institutions, the corporation is "prototypical"—typical not of what exists now but rather of that which will be at some future time. To study the corporate form, therefore, is to speculate on a future America.* From contemporary reality must be extrapolated the trends.

Unlike the religious and guild structures of earlier centuries, the large firm of today has no theoretical rationale linking power, purpose, and responsibility. Indeed, the dilemma is even more fundamental. For there is no satisfactory answer to the first question of all: What is a corporation?

The question centers on the problem of who is represented in the exercise of corporate power, and whether that power is evidenced in politics or any other segment

* This chapter will consider the business corporation, chiefly because it is the chief instrument of economic power and the prime agency for technological development in American society. In fact, the nation's largest firms employ only a minor proportion of the country's labor force. However, the 500 biggest industrial companies provided jobs for about 14 million Americans, or 70 percent of the population working in that sector of the economy in 1969. Moreover, that figure is a substantial advance over a dozen years ago and is actually 1.35 times higher than it was in 1955, when only half were on the top 500 payrolls.

The fastest-growing segment of the work force is in non-business employment: not only agencies at all levels of government but also in a surfeit of non-profit enterprises funded from public and private sources. Many of these organizations are also corporate in structure—universities, foundations, medical centers, research institutes—and thus many of the observations made here apply to them as well as to business firms.

39

of society. Most Americans believe that power should be representative, that the ability to control resources should act in the name of human beings if it is to be legitimate. The corporation, however, is power—the power of productive assets—without a human constituency. It has interests to promote and defend, but they are the interests of a machine more than those of the people who guide, and profit from, the machine's workings. The managers who sit astride the corporate complexes do indeed have power; but it is the power bestowed on them by the resources of the enterprises they tend. Executives come and go, and their terms of office in the top positions are surprisingly short. But the productive assets remain, continually developing new interests to be safeguarded and new demands to be fulfilled.

The increasing irrelevance of people may be illustrated by the role of the stockholder. Approximately a third of all stock purchases are held for less than six months. Thus, an appreciable fraction of those who are the legal owners of corporate America are not ongoing constituents of the firms in which they happen to hold shares but rather transient investors with no sustained interests in the fortunes of the companies bearing the names on their stock certificates.

Nor can it be claimed that a corporation represents its stockholders. This proposition needs little explanation. Legal ownership and effective management have little or nothing to do with one another at the present stage of corporate development. Management recruits its own members with no interference from stockholders, and company policy is made by the men who will carry it out. A large corporation will have over 100 million shares of stock outstanding, and upward of a million owners. Such a dispersion of ownership means that power gravitates to the full-time executives who not only run the company but also make up the agendas for the board of directors' and stockholders' meetings. Furthermore, the individual stockholder attending the annual meeting has power only in proportion to the number of shares he holds. In addition, almost half of the stockholdings in American corporations are held not by people but by other corporate entities. According to a survey taken by the New York Stock Exchange, about half of the outstanding shares were held by fiduciaries, stockbrokers, security dealers, nominees, and institutions. This means that when a vote is taken at an annual meeting, the ballots of the myriad Smiths and Jones and Browns are joined by those of Merrill Lynch and Metropolitan Life and Ford Foundation. Individual stockholders support the existing management out of habit or inertia, while institutional stockholders do so as a matter of considered policy. The upshot is that the acquiescence of individual stockholders combines with the interest of institutional stockholders to give management a free hand.

That power may be rendered legitimate by demonstrating its representative quality has always been one of the foundations of democratic theory. Where power is exercised by—and within—voluntary associations, it can usually be argued that officials are elected by constituents who have consented to the uses of authority and cast equal votes in determining personnel and policies. Authority may be assigned rather than direct, and consent

41

may be tacit rather than active, but the presumption remains that power in public and in private life will have a representative base.

Correlative to this theory is the familiar pluralist model: a society composed of a multiplicity of groups, and a citizenry actively engaged in the associational life. The sociology of democracy adumbrated by James Madison and reiterated by Alexis de Tocqueville is firmly rooted in our thinking. This model presupposes a wide dispersion of power among many interacting and overlapping groups in both society and the political system. Some measure of equilibrium among forces is assumed, and if there is conflict, it results in compromises that do not oppress any of the participants. And the groups with which we are dealing are presumed to be voluntary associations, consisting of individual citizens who join together to further their common interests. Well suited to this scheme are the myriad professional, occupational, religious, and other groups that speak in their members' names. Were groups such as the American Medical Association, the United Automobile Workers, the National Association for the Advancement of Colored People, and the American Legion the only participants in the struggle for political and economic preferment, then the sociology of democracy would continue as a viable theory. For it may still be assumed that, despite tendencies toward bureaucratization, the power of these associations is simply an extension of the interests and wills of their constituent members.

But when General Electric, American Telephone and Telegraph, and Standard Oil of New Jersey enter the pluralist arena, we have elephants dancing among the chickens. For corporate institutions are not voluntary associations of individuals but rather associations of assets, and no theory yet propounded has declared that machines are entitled to a voice in the democratic process. A corporate institution cannot easily claim to have "members." It may profess to speak for its employees, but there is often evidence that not a few on its payroll are quite out of sympathy with the management's policies. It may profess to speak for its stockholders. But many of these are not human beings; and of those who are, a vote is cast for each share owned and not by the conventional democratic standard of one ballot per individual. Neither our constitutional law nor our political theory is able to account for the corporate presence in the arena of social power. Indeed, it is not at all clear by what right the corporation is entitled to power at all. It may well be that discourse will follow reality, that we will find some painless way of rationalizing the arrangements in our midst. But as yet no philosophy has been created which mingles men and machines as joint participants, nor is it clear that American inventive genius will be able to adjust the vocabulary of democracy so as to allow corporate institutions to assume the role of just plain folks.

Corporate Power

Discussions of corporate power tend to be vague, and not a few commentators seem to assume a general agreement that corporate institutions exercise great influence in society. But what, precisely, is the power of the corporation? Power to do what?

The conventional view is that the businessman is far from a free agent. Any executive will wax eloquent on how he is hemmed in on all sides. He will point to a plethora of government agencies, all of which regulate his conduct. There is the Federal Trade Commission, the National Labor Relations Board, the Antitrust Division of the Justice Department, and, of course, the Internal Revenue Service. And then there are labor unions, further limiting his freedom of action. He has customers and suppliers telling him what they want and what he can get; and he has stockholders waiting for dividends, capital gains, and efficient management. And of course there is the ubiquitous consumer who must be satisfied at all stages lest bankruptcy be the consequence. However, the question is not whether businessmen feel hamstrung, for they have objected to their powerlessness since they were first told to buy safety devices for their dangerous machines. The point is whether these limiting factors take on much significance when weighed against the areas of unrestricted freedom of action.

It should be noted at the outset that large corporations do not go bankrupt. They can, as the steel companies have demonstrated, be inefficient, and still be profitable. Their relative share of the market can rise or fall, and their rank in the industry may change slightly over the years, but mergers and reorganizations keep the assets and production facilities intact. To be sure, a corporation must make its decisions with an eye on profit. But in the highest circles the concern is with the growth of the

44

enterprise over several decades, and profits are but a means to this end. The real issue is how autonomous these enterprises are and what are the consequences of their decisions for society as a whole. What, in short, can corporations do with the power they are alleged to have?

Despite an occasional outburst from the White House, corporate managers can administer prices as they see fit. They are not required to submit proposed increases to any government agency for approval. They may ask what the market will bear, and, generally speaking, the market will pay what is asked. Stockholders have accustomed themselves to a modest dividend, and this is usually passed on to them without discussion. Top management maintains a suitable level of earnings by its ability to set prices. In addition, it decides what proportion of the earnings will go to the stockholders and what proportion is to be retained by the company. Wages are, of course, subject to collective bargaining. But this process simply maintains the status quo. For wage increases just about keep pace with increases in productivity, and the share of a corporation's income which goes to wages remains about the same over the years. Management has even more freedom in determining salaries. Here it can determine who is to become wealthy and how great this wealth is to be. Decisions on executive compensation, in particular, go far toward determining aspirations for an entire society. The purchasing power bestowed on the men at and near the top makes for a style of life which becomes a goal for those lower down on the pyramid.

The large corporations shape the material contours of the nation's life. While original ideas for new products

45

may come from a variety of sources, it is the big companies that have the resources to bring these goods to the public. The argument that the consumer has "free will," deciding what he will and will not buy, can be taken just so far. For in actual fact we *do* buy much or even most of what the large corporations put on the shelves or in the showrooms for us.

Companies are not unsophisticated, and they have a fair idea of what the consumer will be willing to purchase. But the general rule, with fewer exceptions than we would like to think, is that if they make it, we will buy it. Thus, we air-condition our bedrooms, watch color television in our living rooms, brush our teeth electrically in the bathroom, and cook at eye level in the kitchen. It is time for frankness on this score: the American consumer is not notable for imagination and does not know what he "wants." Thus, he waits for corporate America to develop new products and, on hearing of them, discovers a long-felt "need" he never knew he had. What should be noted is that the number and character of a man's possessions have a singular impact on the personality of their owner. Materialism is not uniquely American, nor is the high valuation placed on material possessions entirely the result of management decisions. However, the perpetuation of this system of values, with its stress on tangible possessions and labor-saving devices, is due to corporate judgment about what sales are needed if rates and turnover of production are to be kept at the optimum level.

And more than any other single force in society, the large corporations govern the character and quality of the nation's labor market. The most visible example of this prowess has been the decision of companies to introduce computers into the world of work, bringing an unmistakable message to those who must earn a living. Millions of Americans are being told what skills they will have to possess if they are to fill the jobs that will be available. A company, whether its product happens to be power mowers or life insurance or air transportation, has the freedom to decide *how* it will produce its goods and services. And having made this decision, it establishes its recruiting patterns accordingly. Individuals must tailor themselves to the job if they want to work at all. Most of us and all of our children will find ourselves adjusting to new styles of work whether we want to or not.

The impact of corporate organization and technology on the American educational system deserves far closer attention than it has been given. Whether we are talking of a vocational high school in Los Angeles or an engineering college in Milwaukee or a law school in New Haven, the curriculum is largely determined by the job needs of our corporate enterprises. The message goes out that certain kinds of people having certain kinds of knowledge are needed. All American education, in a significant sense, is vocational. Liberal-arts students may enjoy a period of insulation, but they are well aware that eventually they will have to find niches for themselves in offices or laboratories.

Corporate managements are free to decide where they will locate their plants and offices. This power has also contributed, probably more than anything else, to the suburban explosion, for the white-collar class must have a place to live. A handful of executives decides which parts of the country are to prosper and which are to stagnate. If over half the counties in the United States lose population each decade, this is largely because corporate managements are unwilling to locate facilities in areas they consider unsuitable. On the other hand, regions the corporations do favor experience a radical transformation. New citizens move in and old values must adjust themselves to new influences. Cities and towns, while welcoming branch plants as sources of jobs and revenue, find that what were once local decisions are now made from the outside and by outsiders. Moreover, as corporations expand across the nation, they turn many of their white-collar employees into transients who are prepared to leave as management beckons them to new job opportunities. The nomadic life has consequences for family and personality which are not without disturbing qualities.

The regions that have not prospered in postwar years have been those where corporations have opted not to situate. Too much can be made of the New England "ghost towns." Actually, corporations have "pulled out" of very few places; more critical has been their failure to establish or expand facilities in alternative parts of the country. Thus, patterns of migration—from the countryside to the city and from the city to the suburb—are reflections of corporate decisions on plant and office location.

Related to this have been the corporate decisions to locate their firms' headquarters in the center of our largest cities, especially the East Side of New York. Leaving aside the architectural transformation with which we will have to live for many years, the very existence of these prestige palaces has drawn hundreds of thousands of people into metropolitan areas not equipped to handle them. Thus have come not only the traffic snarls and the commuter crush, but also the pyramiding of suburbs for the young-marrieds of management and the thin-walled city apartments for others in their twenties, fifties, and sixties.

Perhaps it has been said too often that ours is an age of "organization men." Yet there is more than a germ of truth in this depiction of the new white-collar class that is rapidly becoming the largest segment of the American population. The great corporations molded this type of individual, and the habits and style of life of corporate employment continue to play a key role in setting values and aspirations for the population as a whole. Working for a large organization has a subtle effect on a person's character. It calls for the virtues of adaptability, sociability, and that certain caution necessary when one knows one is forever being judged.

The type of success represented by a senior engineer at Western Electric or a branch manager for Metropolitan Life is now the model for millions. Not only does the prestige of the corporation rub off on the employee, but he seems to be riding an escalator that can only move upward. Too much can be made of the alleged "repudiation" of business and corporate life by the current generation of college students. This may be the case at Swarthmore, Oberlin, and in certain ivied circles. But the great majority of undergraduates—who are, after all, at places like Penn State and Purdue—would like nothing better than a good berth in Ford or Texaco. Indeed, they

49

are even now priming themselves to become the sort of person those companies will want them to be.

The pervasive influence of the large corporations derives less from how many people they employ than from their great wealth. Our largest firms have a good deal of spare cash to spend where they like. These companies make profits almost automatically every year, and they find it necessary to give only a fraction of those earnings to their stockholders in the form of dividends.*

Thus, the big firms have had the money to create millions of new white-collar jobs. Department heads in the large companies ask for and are assigned additional assistants, coordinators, planners, and programmers who fill up new acres of office space every year. And everyone appears to keep busy: attending meetings and conferences, flying around the country, and writing and reading and amending memoranda.

That a large proportion of these employees are not necessary was illustrated when, due to a long labor dispute, one large corporation took the unprecedented step of firing one-third of its white-collar force. The wholesale departure of these clerks and executives had no effect on the company's production and sales. Nevertheless, the company was not one to show that an empire could function half-clothed, and it hired back the office workers it did not need just as soon as the cash was again available.

If all this sounds a bit like Alice in Wonderland, it would be well to ponder on what the consequences

---

* Quite clearly, the biggest corporations stand no risk of going out of business. Of the firms ranking among the top 40 a dozen years ago, all but two are still in pre-eminent positions. And the pair that slipped continue to remain in the top 100.

50

would be if all our major corporations cut their white-collar staffs to only those who were actually needed. Could the nation bear the resulting unemployment, especially involving so many people who have been conditioned to believe that they possess special talents and qualities of character?

Corporate wealth, then, is spent as a corporation wishes. If General Motors wants to tear down the Savoy-Plaza Hotel in New York City and erect a headquarters for itself at Fifth Avenue and 59th Street, it will go ahead and do so. An office building could, at a quarter of the cost, have been located at Eleventh Avenue and 17th Street. But why should cost be the prime consideration? After all, the stockholders have received their dividends, new production facilities have been put into operation, and there is still plenty of money left over. Nor is such a superfluity of spare cash limited to the very largest concerns. Ford, which is generally thought of as General Motors' poor sister, was sufficiently well heeled to drop a quarter of a billion dollars on its Edsel design and still not miss a dividend.

Management alone decides when to invest—in new capital equipment, in new locations, in new processes, products, and personnel. It need not receive the approval of any governmental agency, and no such agency can compel a corporation to go ahead with an investment program if it feels like retrenching. While top executives will be attuned to expectations of the public's buying, it can just as well shape these expectations by announcing a buoyant expansion program. The good will of investors need not be courted, as large corporations can use their retained earnings for investment purposes. And there is increasing reliance on the huge investing institutions—insurance companies, pension funds, banks, brokerage houses—for funds. Representatives of these institutions sit on or are close to the boards of the large corporations and are really part of the corporate circle. Together they decide how and in what amounts capital will be invested over the decades to come. The power to make investment decisions is concentrated in a few hands, and it is this power which will decide what kind of a nation America will be. Instead of government planning there is boardroom planning that is accountable to no outside agency: and these plans set the order of priorities on national growth, technological innovation, and, ultimately, the values and behavior of human beings. Investment decisions are sweeping in their ramifications—no one is unaffected by their consequences. Yet this is an area where neither the public nor its government is able to participate. If the contours of the economy and the society are being shaped in a few score boardrooms, these decisions, so far as the average citizen is concerned, are in the lap of the gods.

Corporate Technology

Since no public agencies need give their approval to investment decisions, government is unable to control technological advances, no matter how much these promise to change the face of society.* And it must be

---

* If the corporation has presided over the technological development of American society, this is because capital development in the

underlined that this power is the power of men only at the margin. For the managers who make the decisions on behalf of the machines are their servants rather than their masters. No human conspiracy can be held accountable for the decisions that are taken. The machines are the prime movers, but they cannot be held to account. Like all material objects, they have momentum but no morality.

Only a few decades ago scientists and engineers, working in the Bell laboratories of the American Telephone and Telegraph Corporation, developed the transistor. No immutable laws predestined this device to emerge from the minds and hands of those particular men, at that precise moment. What was inevitable, however, was the eventual development of a contrivance like a transistor. Its emergence was the inescapable "next step" in the progress of industrial technology in America.

Once developed, the transistor became an effective component of the nation's productive machine. Ideas inspiring invention can emanate from a wide variety of sources, many of them quite unprepossessing. But today industrial development follows invention only if financial underwriting can be found. A generous supply of finance capital—especially from the treasuries of large

United States is not a governmental function. Industrial innovation can, of course, occur in state laboratories, and financial underwriting can come from public sources. This is what happens in collectivist countries. But America is capitalist, not collectivist; and for this reason technological imperatives must be discussed in the context of corporate investment. Moreover, many of the remarks made here concerning technology's impact would remain valid even if state functionaries made the decisions on capital allocation and investment priorities.

corporations—has turned countless inventions into productive reality. While in one sense the executives of the telephone company made the "decision" to invest hundreds of millions of dollars in the transistor's development, it is more meaningful to acknowledge that a significant technological breakthrough carries with it its own decision. The transistor's coming into existence, combined with the fact that it could be made cheaply and in large quantities, was sufficient to assure financial underwriting. There are occasions when patents can be suppressed for a period, but there are also times—and the transistor came along at such a time—when men have no option but to do the bidding of the machines they have created.

The transistor soon made feasible a whole range of opportunities. The electronic computer could now be developed. (There could have been a pre-transistor computer, but even the simplest model would have had to be the size of an apartment house.) And with the computer would come a new array of machines, ranging from missiles to automated assembly lines. The most highly placed politicians and policy-makers would be obliged to reorient their thinking about global strategy. Thousands of warehouse workers, deprived of jobs because they were no longer needed to take inventory, would be forced to recast their lives. Millions of small children would learn new forms of arithmetic because the new machines would be part of their adult years.

And man's knowledge of himself and of his external world would take on new forms, orienting itself to the types of information the machines could develop and process. Not only does a computer assemble new pyramids of data, but it demands that those utilizing its output accommodate themselves to its logic. The categories of the human mind which give us our perceptions and interpretations of reality are not independent or discretionary artifacts. They come into being because thought must be disciplined, and the order imposed on the mind is less of our own making than the product of social circumstances. Whereas a logic devised by a Descartes or a Kant might serve the needs of students and scholars of earlier periods, now machines have appeared to shape the outlines of the classifications and formulas whereby knowledge itself is developed. Our images of space, of society, of the mind itself are more and more being filtered through the categories of machines that intervene between us and the external world.

Another, quite different, illustration may provide further clarity. In a short time it will be technologically feasible to manufacture and distribute a cheap and easily administered birth-control compound, certainly one less expensive than those now available and without suspicious side-effects—perhaps an injection a man may take once a year or a pill a woman can use after sexual intercourse. And once such a device becomes easily attainable, its use will soon become customary in all sectors of society. For a time some couples may elect to enter each other's arms unarmored by contraceptive protection; but within a generation the question of "choice" will be virtually academic. Just as churches are now air-conditioned—even though God intended us to swelter in the summer—so will sexual values adjust themselves to the facts of a new technology. Those inclined to stress continuity will explain that our basic morality has not really changed—that traditional principles have only undergone adjustment as they confront changed conditions. Publicists and theologians will call for a reassessment of pre-pill rules of behavior; and after the predictable battles between tradition and innovation, a revised morality will become the new orthodoxy. The ethics of a society adapt to technological facts, and it is the business of moralists to pick up their ideological pieces as best they can.

Given convenient contraception, the alterations in society will be sweeping. Family relations, the role of women, the character of mating and marriage, relations between races and classes, notions of right and wrong—all these conditions will change without a people's having planned or given consent to the new arrangements with which they will be compelled to live.

Yet men have a certain pride—founded more on the hopes they nurture than on their record of experience—making them affirm their ability to control their environment. It would be foolish to argue that such control has never been achieved: floods, famine, and plague have been prevented, occasional economic crises have been anticipated and lessened, even wars have been forestalled—but all this is at the margin. The chief movements of society, the significant patterns of social change, even those developments we call "progress," all possess a momentum and a direction of their own. The role of chance, of the coincidence of opportunities, is paramount. When invention and capital converge, the face of a society will undergo a transformation, no matter how much men may argue or protest over the consequences.

The movements of technology are not matters of social policy or human choice.

No conscious or purposeful decision to develop steam power or electricity or the internal-combustion engine was ever made by men. More important, it is no longer possible to decide *against* developing such a machine when the opportunity to develop one is at hand. Of no society can it be said that its inhabitants have decided, once the resources were available, to leave an incipient technology on the drawing board. Men emerge, attracted as if by a larger-than-life magnet, to build and operate the new machines. At one stage in history those men may be free-booting entrepreneurs; at another they will be ruthless commissars or anonymous bureaucrats. But everyone, owners and managers no less than the humblest peasant who quits the fields to toil in a factory, is drawn along the new paths of employment and opportunity.

The men and women of all societies, in their personalities and habits and expectations, reflect their relation to the machines characterizing their age. If this was the radical historiography of Karl Marx, it was also a fact of life well understood by such conservatives as Alexis de Tocqueville and Alexander Hamilton. This is not to postulate that man and his nature are infinitely manipulable. It is rather to acknowledge that the varieties in human character the world has known have in largest measure been shaped by the productive processes existing or emerging in a particular age. The farmer who guides a metal plow is a different order of man from the farmer who rides atop a diesel-powered combine. The stoker in an engine cab is a man distinct from the pilot in a supersonic jet. The bookkeeper stooped over an ink-stained ledger differs from the computer programmer in a glass-and-aluminum palace. Indeed, the woman who takes a daily contraceptive pill is a totally different person from the woman who leaves procreation to chance.

All talk of character and personality, of human freedom and responsibility, of the options to do with one's life as one pleases, fades into insignificance when technology's impact on society is measured. We are what we are because machines have defined the alternatives available to us. We choose—if the notion of choice can be used at all—the course of comfort, of security, of least resistance. That men have always opted for comfort and security may be one of the few immutables of human nature. Certainly, if given the opportunity, men will ride rather than walk, labor with their hands rather than with their backs, have two or three children rather than five or six. And as the machine beckons us, as it takes easy advantage of our desire for ease and efficiency, so we follow.

While fully aware of the objections to such a thesis, I must conclude that the major contours of a society and the experience of life known by its inhabitants are determined by its technology more than by any other factor. Once the instruments are on their way toward development, men will emerge to work with those artifacts, and it becomes meaningless to speculate on whether the adjustments they make in their lives have been voluntary or involuntary.

58

The Corporate Elite

From these observations at least one conclusion is possible: an "elite" presides over corporate America. Yet it must be understood that the "elite" in question consists not so much of identifiable personalities (how many of the presidents of our twenty largest corporations can any of us name?) but rather of the chairs in the top offices.

The typical corporation head stays at his desk for less than ten years. The power he exercises is less discretionary than we would like to believe, and the range of decisions that can be called uniquely his own is severely limited. (It is only in the small companies on the way up that the top men impress their personalities on the enterprise.) When a corporation president retires and his successor is named, the price of the company's stock, presumably a barometer of informed opinion, does not change perceptibly.

The top managers of the largest companies do not gather at scheduled intervals to make their key decisions in concert. At the same time, it is clear that they know what is on one another's minds. Whether they come together casually at their clubs or hunting lodges, or slightly more formally at the Business Council or the Committee for Economic Development or the Foreign Policy Association, they are definitely not isolated from each other. Informal conversation elicits plans, hopes, expectations. There is a community of interest and sentiment among this elite, and any thought of a "conspiracy" is both invalid and irrelevant. Moreover, the critical investment decisions bring together many members of the elite—executives, bankers, brokers—and the decision to expand or retrench is clearly based on consultation and agreement. Such decisions are made with the knowledge of what others are doing or plan to do. The lines of communication are built into the system.

Nor is the corporate elite a "class," any more than the corporate world is "capitalist" in the classical sense. The members of the elite come from a variety of backgrounds, or at least from every segment of the middle class. Birth and upbringing are of negligible importance, and promotion to the highest corporate circles is based on talent more than on manners or connections. Those in the elite group are simply the men who sit in particular chairs at any particular time; the chairs, rather than their occupants, have the power. Thus, there is little point in discussing "who" has the power unless one explores the sources of that power. This needs to be stressed because there is strong reason to believe that the institutional structure determines the behavior of the men who hold positions in it and that it does not really matter who the officeholders are as individuals.

The top men in the top companies are symbolic of a new breed of American. Their distinction lies in having passed the stringent tests by which our society determines who will rise to its heights and who will be left behind. Every modern organization has multiple hurdles, and the route to the top for an archbishop, a four-star general, or a university chancellor has a great deal in common with that traveled by a corporation president.

Career success today is based on talent and what is especially rewarded is ability and willingness to devote one's talents to goals chosen not by oneself but by others.

The future corporation president can emerge from anywhere in the generous bosom of the American middle class. All that companies ask, in their initial recruitment of potential executives, is that a young man possess a college diploma. It doesn't matter where he went to school, and in most cases no one cares who his father was or what he did for a living. Among the top executives of today there are more products of the Big Ten than of the Ivy League, and in the corporate circles of the future it is clear that graduates of Purdue will far outnumber those from Princeton.

The president of one large corporation was born in Lolo, Montana (population 235), and went on to Montana State University. Itasca, Texas; Walton, Kentucky; Hattiesburg, Mississippi; and Shelby, Nebraska produced local boys who made it to the top ranks of Gulf Oil, North American Aviation, Texaco, and the Ford Motor Company. Very few of today's top executives went to private preparatory schools, and hardly more than three or four out of a hundred are listed in the metropolitan Social Registers.

The open-eyed young man, first taken on as a technician of one sort or another, soon discovers what is wanted if he is to distinguish himself from his classmates. This is the comprehension that he is, above all else, working in and for a business. The up-and-comer soon learns to think first in business terms: the specialized skills he was taught at college are useful only if they can be ap-

61

plied to augmenting the firm's earnings. At a certain point he may have to compromise with professional standards in making or promoting a profitable but less-than-quality product. How he reacts to this challenge will be noted by his superiors.

By the time he is in his early thirties, the man-on-the-way-up will have left his old friends behind at their account books and drafting boards. He is now manager of a large department or perhaps a branch plant. The best indication of his early success is that he now has as subordinates men older than himself; not only has he passed his peers but he has bypassed some who were once ahead of him. What is required now is the top-management look, usually achieved by emulating the appearance and outlook of one's immediate and remote superiors. It is generally an air of taciturn tough-mindedness, an impression of deliberate decisiveness. Those who undergo such a transformation do so not deliberately but as an unconscious adaptation.

The executive personality can probably be mastered more easily by the boy from Itasca than by the graduate of Groton. The corporate graces are, on the whole, those of middle-class life in Detroit or Chicago. In contrast to his European counterparts, the American executive does not have to know wines and is actually a step ahead if he prefers his steak without sauce Béarnaise. What is needed most in these years is ambition, drive, willingness to make company business the center of his life. The difficulty is that this test comes at just the wrong time. His children are in high school and faced with all the problems of adolescence; his wife is beginning to feel the passing of the years and starts to wonder just where she stands in his diffused affections. But at this period he must bring work home every night—except those nights when he is traveling to a trade-association meeting in San Francisco, to a commission hearing in Washington, to merger negotiations in Chicago, or simply to see what has gone wrong at the assembly plant in Shreveport.

No one can assert with complete confidence that the fourteen-hour day is absolutely necessary for high-quality executive performance. Walter Bagehot once observed that businessmen work much too hard for their own good, with the result that they make a lot of money in the morning and then, instead of stopping when they're ahead, proceed to lose half of it in the afternoon. However, if the sheep are to be separated from the goats, certain rituals must be enforced and observed. One corporation chairman calls frequent Sunday-morning meetings just to see which of his vice-presidents grumble.

During this period, also, a presidential contender will have to become something of a philosopher. Thus the need to affirm that the economy is the central institution of the society, that business profit is the prime mover in the nation's life. He will, moreover, come to believe that whatever it is his company produces is absolutely necessary for the well-being of the American citizen-consumer. He must take the view—and this attitude cannot be faked—that the six-sided frozen French-fried potato is an asset to the nation's dinner table; that automobile exhaust is not really responsible for air pollution; that his firm is doing all it can to give jobs to blacks and school drop-outs. For only if such sentiments are uttered with a ring of inner conviction will he be adjudged a true company man.

A man's fate can be shaped by whether the special area of interest he developed many years ago turns out to be a critical one for the corporation at the time when the penultimate promotions are being made. There appears, then, to be a semi-deterministic "Law of Strategic Talents," accelerating the rise of individuals who have skills that unexpectedly take on central significance. Nevertheless, it would be a mistake to counsel an ambitious young man, now entering college, on how to equip himself for the semi-finals of 1995. Advice that he prepare himself for computerized investment programming or psychoanalytic labor relations could well be an act of misguidance. For just when he is ready for the final round, the company may discover that consumer resistance has returned and the top job may be given to an old-fashioned sales type who has the unscientific knack of making people want to take out their checkbooks. There are, as the sages keep telling us, some things that just can't be planned.

All things considered, the American corporation has become a self-selecting, self-contained civil service. The men at the top of corporate America undergo far less criticism than the average senator or governor, in part because they don't have to face popular elections and in part because the ideology of private ownership insulates them from public scrutiny. It may well be that the time has come to alter outdated assumptions about the presumed "private" character of our major corporations. By any reasonable measure AT&T is as important an institution in American society as the state of Alabama, and the presiding officer of that company deserves as much attention as the governor of that state. Corporation executives are not very interesting people, however, and not the least reason is that they have had to become bland in order to get where they are.

It would be wrong to call these men conservatives, for once again the conventional language of ideology does not apply here. Many of the decisions they make, whether so intended or not, have revolutionary consequences for all of society. The technological and marketing transformations they have effected have given a new shape to postwar America, and the plans they are making for the remainder of the century may alter the face of the nation beyond recognition.*

The men who preside over American corporations are chiefly of unpretentious origins, and they have won a race where there is room at the finish line for only a few. At no time in their trials were they expected to display humane learning, any more than a philosophy professor is asked to show a profit for his department. The job of an employee is to protect the interests of his employer, even if that employer is an abstract combination of assets called a corporation. Most corporation presidents would not even belabor the theory that what is good for General Electric or General Dynamics is good for the country. Their job is to look out for the good of their company.

---

* While it is amusing to reflect on the horse-and-buggy values of a man like Henry Ford, his real role was to hurtle the nation into an era that would be incapable of adhering to earlier standards. The philosophical pronouncements of businessmen receive far too much attention; the decisions they make while doing their jobs are the important catalysts of social change.

65

This should not be taken as criticism. Most of these men have invested their energy and ardor in a particular line of endeavor. To expect that our corporations will somehow produce an aristocratic order is, to misunderstand important conditions that have accompanied recent changes in the structure of American life. It is futile, then, to wish that our corporate managers underwent more instruction in moral philosophy or modern sociology. During most of their formative years, the exigencies of the climb force them to think of themselves rather than for themselves. This is an inevitable consequence of opening careers to the talented, of breaking down the barriers that once prevented men of inauspicious background from rising to the top.

Not only corporations but universities and medical centers, foundations and research institutes, government agencies and the military establishment are recruiting and shaping individuals to serve their needs and eventually fill their top positions. The making of the nation's corporate elite is more than a success story. Its greater significance is as part of the natural history of our time, wherein men perceive what is wanted of them and then pattern their lives to meet these specifications.

Corporate Capitalism

If our large corporations are using their power to reshape American society, the general public's thinking about such concentrated influence still remains ambiguous. There persist, for example, the ideology of anti-

trust and the fond place in American hearts still occupied by small business. Thus, politicians can count on
striking a resonant chord when they call for more vigorous prosecutions under the Sherman Law and for greater
appropriations for the Small Business Administration.
Most Americans do agree, from time to time, that our
largest companies are too big and should somehow be
broken up into smaller units. But just how strong or enduring this sentiment is is hard to say. No one really expects that Mobil Oil or Bethlehem Steel can or will be
"busted" into ten or a dozen entirely new and independent companies. Thus, if the ideology that bigness equals
badness lingers on, there is no serious impetus to translate
that outlook into action.

Part of the problem is that if Americans are suspicious
of bigness, they do not really know what it is about large
corporations which troubles them. Despite the periodic
exposures of defective brake cylinders or profiteering on
polio vaccine, the big story is not really one of callous
exploitation or irresponsibility. Given the American system of values, it is difficult to mount a thoroughgoing
examination of capitalism or to be "anti-business" in an
unequivocal way. The result is that our commentaries in
this area are piecemeal and sporadic. We have the vocabularies for criticizing "big government" and "big labor,"
but the image of the large corporation is a hazy one, and
despite its everyday presence in our midst, our reaction
to its very existence is uncertain.

The American corporate system continues, in major
outlines, to be capitalist in structure. Talk of a welfare
state, of a mixed economy, even of a managerial revolu-

tion is of limited utility, for the fact remains that major decisions in the economy are private. They are made within closed circles, and public agencies cannot intrude in any effective way. Corporate capitalism of course differs from classical capitalism, but the transformation has been only in the adjective—not the noun. This is why reform is so difficult. Can the private managers of corporate capital be made institutionally responsible to the public? Accountability seems impossible in the American framework. Experience has thus far shown that public agencies set up to regulate private enterprise are soon brought to a close sympathy with the industries they are supposed to be regulating. This should occasion no great surprise. Corporations are powerful, and they will use their resources to maintain a climate favorable to themselves. While in the realm of pure logic a Federal Power Commission in Washington might tell Standard Oil of California what it might or might not do, in actual fact such an agency is less powerful than the corporation. Similarly, our ideology permits us to rest happy in the thought that the Anti-Trust Division of the Justice Department could "break up" General Dynamics or International Business Machines into collections of separate companies. The fact of power, however, is that this has not been done and cannot be done because government is weaker than the corporate institutions purportedly subordinate to it. This is the politics of capitalism. It is expressive not of a conspiracy but rather of a harmony of political forms and economic interests on a plane determined by the ongoing needs of corporate institutions.

Are there alternatives to corporate capitalism? Few

voices are heard suggesting the public ownership of major industries, and it is just as well, for the odds are that nationalization would end in disillusion. The problem is that there is no real middle ground. This was known to both Adam Smith and Karl Marx, but it is a fact hard to swallow in an age that seeks reason along the course of moderation. Suppose that America followed the British pattern and nationalized a few industries such as railroads, electricity, and the coal mines. Instead of becoming agencies of the public interest, these industries would soon enter service as handmaidens of the private sector of the economy. For the preponderance of economic power remaining in corporate hands would ensure that the industries in the public sector were suitably docile and did not serve as vehicles for serious planning that might jeopardize corporate interests. In short, partial nationalization would not make economic decisions accountable to the public but would create yet another set of official agencies to be captured by corporate enterprise.

On the other hand, the state could nationalize all industry, thus once and for all destroying private economic power. This was and is the Marxian prescription, offered with the full understanding that the old order must be felled with one stroke if the new is to rise from its ashes. But the problems of irresponsibility in corporate America are minor compared with those of totalitarianism, and the Marxist alternative to capitalism is hardly one that those who have known a free society will embrace with enthusiasm.

Hence the frustrations that mark any search for a

middle ground. We hear much of regulation, of intervention, of planning on the part of government. But
who, for example, are to be the planners? What is to be
their source of power, as against their legal authority,
and who will give force to their decisions? And is it possible to prevent corporate institutions from seducing,
capturing, and otherwise infiltrating those who are man-
dated to plan the economy in the public interest? Until
such questions are answered, the power of corporate
America will continue to grow, and in directions of its
own choosing.

The Corporate Constituency

At the same time that the corporate presence is making
its weight felt on the larger society, an increasing section
of the population is enlisting itself in the service of these
institutions. Corporate employment is on the rise, particularly through its creation of new white-collar jobs, with
the consequence that millions of Americans are experiencing styles of work and modes of life unknown to
earlier generations.

Those on corporate white-collar payrolls are still a minority of the labor force, but they are significant if only
because they demonstrate how employment in a particular setting affects the lives of individuals. If the prospect
of a corporate career spells new opportunities, the decision to enter this protective shelter also entails the
payment of certain prices. In actual fact the vast majority of those who join the middle-class cadre of corporate

institutions are freer, happier, and more secure than any similar group in the nation's history. And if to gain these benefactions they have had to adapt their personalities to new norms of behavior, it is a condition that was gladly met. Thus, the reason for analyzing the society of the corporation is not to celebrate or deplore its way of functioning but rather to describe the effect of that environment on the character of its members. For such an inquiry goes beyond corporate life: it also suggests the kind of people that more and more Americans are going to be.

The corporation has become a social system in a more profound sense than ever before because its members are in greater need of the social satisfactions the corporation can provide. If they seem to enjoy the life that their company provides for them and if they endow it with an ethical sanction, they ought not to be condemned out of hand for violating the creed of a former age. They are not necessarily made of less stern stuff than their fathers. The man without an enterprise of his own must work for someone else; the man who has broken old attachments must find new ties wherever he can.

The white-collar employee of the corporation possesses status as well as contract, for the corporation has begun to assume rather broad obligations toward him, regardless of his value to—or even his performance in—the company. The member of a contract system is regarded simply as an employee whose contract with his employer lasts as long as he does his job. The member of a status system is regarded as a person: the benefits he receives stem less from his performance as an employee than from his stature as an individual.

In a transformed society, managers and workers alike are uprooted, but it is the former—the middle class—who seek adjustment and new roots because of the profound changes they have undergone in environment, expectations, and status. Eastman Kodak's medical plans, IBM's country clubs, Richfield Oil's model homes, du Pont's psychiatrists, Reynolds Tobacco's chaplains, and even RCA's neckties with the corporate insignia—all are symptomatic of the effort to establish a feeling of community within the corporation. The middle-class employee no longer has an alternative community in which he can find a sense of belonging. The national government is too large and unwieldy to provide this satisfaction; and local governments are too ineffectual to cater to such deep-seated needs. Government provides various welfare services at various levels, but they are far from being programs that will meet the social and psychological needs of the middle class.

Thus there has emerged the equivalent of a new kind of citizenship: corporate citizenship. It is not the same as our traditional view of citizenship, which applied to one's residence in a specific town or section of the country and, in a formal sense, also to the individual's relation to his government. Thus, it is important that we understand the political implications of corporate citizenship.

In politics this white-collar class tends to consume what is given to it rather than help to produce the product. The participation of its members is confined, by and large, to voting in the more publicized elections. It is true that the residents of the suburbs vote with great gusto in the big quadrennial elections: the percentage turnouts in the belts around our great cities almost rival the British in their proportions. Yet the vote, it should not be necessary to say, is the barest minimum of political participation; and, apart from the Presidential contests—staffed and directed by people other than themselves—the members of the new middle class stay outside of political activity. They look upon politics as news to be consumed, a drama to be watched. They have none of the sense of political commitment which was second nature to the middle class of previous generations.

Outwardly the new middle class seems content with corporate citizenship and is not bothered by the fact that political affairs are in the hands of others. Yet is this really the case? Studies of the new suburbia show that neurosis and feelings of helplessness are endemic; a sense of isolation and powerlessness is having profound social and psychological effects. Problems of mental health cannot be cured by political participation, but the democratic theory has always assumed that self-government can create the environment in which mental and moral health are most likely to flourish. The middle class, in divorcing itself from politics and making itself dependent on the largess of corporate institutions, has weakened itself immeasurably. If a crisis arises, even a relatively mild one, can we be sure that this group will continue to adhere to democratic values?

These individuals lack the defenses that protected the old middle class. Indeed, the new middle-class citizens created by and absorbed into the corporate structure are dependent on the continued good will of the organiza-

73

tions employing them and are riding the crest of a wave not of their own making. The members of this class feel free, for they are enjoying opportunities their parents never experienced; and their dependent status as employees does not appear a barrier to personal expression and development. Many may be riding for an eventual fall, for it is by no means certain that there will always be secure corporate berths for all desiring them. America's corporate middle class may well be a luxury, possible at present because resources are available for their salaries and positions. But so long as the funds are there to support them, they themselves are persuaded that they are doing useful work. It would be dangerous to society if they were declared superfluous. Such an eventuality is all the more worrisome as white-collar employees, unlike their brothers in blue collars, are psychologically unprepared for the loss of protection and status following unemployment. Were all the white-collar water to be wrung out of the corporate world, it is unlikely that government programs could create face-saving occupations in the numbers required. There would be every likelihood of political repercussions that would test the foundations of corporate capitalism as never before.

The new middle class has thus far found higher incomes and enhanced status, economic security and interesting work in the coroprate world. To them society appears rational, and they have few problems that can specifically be called "public" or "political." If this constituency of the corporation were able to embrace the whole working population, then, despite the increased concentration of power, it could at least be suggested

74

that corporate America was bestowing its largess upon all. But this is not the case.

Unincorporated Americans

There are losers as well as winners in the growth of corporate organization and technology. Not all who work for corporations have secure, let alone ascending, careers. The unskilled and the untrained continue to be hired at hourly wages, and then only for those hours when their services are required. Many of the unemployed are, indeed, corporate unemployed: they have been laid off from jobs they once had with corporations or have not been hired for jobs that corporate technology has been able to abolish. By the same token, trade unions are in a relative stage of decline, a development at least partly to be attributed to technological innovations that have swelled the proportion of white-collar workers in the employed population. Indirectly, and to some extent directly, corporate decisions have, therefore, both increased unemployment and diminished the role of unions. The latter consequence is a serious blow to the doctrine of social pluralism, for organized labor has been traditionally counted upon as a source of countervailing force against the strength of corporate management. The weakening of the unions deprives society of another check to the power of the corporation.

It may well be that two Americas are emerging, one a society protected by the corporate umbrella and the other a society whose members have failed to affiliate themselves with the dominant institutions. This second America will in part consist of small businessmen and other independent spirits who manage to do well without corporate attachments. But, more importantly, it will be comprised of superfluous Americans: the unemployed, the ill-educated, the entire residue of human beings who are not needed by the corporate machine. Little thought has been given to these people. How are they to earn their living? How will they maintain their sense of self-esteem? If this pool grows to substantial proportions, if it finds effective leadership, if it gives vent to its resentments—then, and perhaps then only, will a force arise to challenge the great corporate institutions. For then will power meet power, the power of a mass movement confronting the power of the machine. The discard heap that the machine created may arise to devour its progenitor.

This revolution—with or without violence, whether from the left or from the right—will be averted only if corporate America can make room in its environs for those who demand entry. Has it the jobs, the resources, the will, and the imagination to achieve this? Thus far, corporate America has escaped open attack because the victims of new technology do not yet outnumber its beneficiaries. But technology advances according to rules of its own, and loyalty to now-dominant institutions may diminish if accelerated automation or economic reverses reduce the corporate constituency. In this event, this second America, the society of losers, may grow in numbers and power with increasing rapidity. The resolution will not be a pleasant one.

4: Superfluous Americans

THE POSTWAR YEARS have been generous to Americans who wear the badge of productive persons. The sole requirement for such status is gainful employment: holding a job can be construed as evidence of having contributed to society's well-being. To be sure, many jobs serve no useful purpose; nevertheless, the test of self-support demands only that a person be paid a wage for doing something—or simply being present at a specified place over a designated period of time. The majority of Americans have found themselves equal to this relatively undemanding assignment, thus endowing their presence with civic legitimacy. Moreover, wives and offspring of wage-earning husbands enjoy auxiliary membership in productive America; even if they produce no wealth, affiliation with someone who does permits them to share the honorific status.

77

Unfortunately, not everyone can be productive. Indeed, the facts suggest that the proportion of unproductive people has been rising in recent years. Yet the heart of the problem lies not so much with the unemployed and unemployable as in the attitude taken toward those who cannot pull their economic weight. While there is general agreement that these Americans must be supported by the productive segments of society, the granting of such assistance requires its recipients to assume a subordinate form of citizenship. For they are superfluous people: human beings for whom the nation has no need.

The American economy cannot assimilate the entire population. The system as a whole reaches the point of equilibrium—optimum profits and the most efficient use of capital—without having to employ everyone who needs to or would like to work. There are no longer jobs available for adolescents and the aged, for the under-educated and the infirm. There was a time when our farms and factories could employ virtually everyone, even if some of the tasks performed were modest and only marginally remunerative. Today, however, only about two-thirds of all Americans have effective membership in the economy, either through full-time employment or via affiliation with a working husband or father. Neither classical economics nor Keynesian theory anticipated a national economy embracing so delimited a segment of the population. Moreover, lack of jobs for those willing and able to work is only part of the problem. For the great majority of those excluded from the economy are, by contemporary standards, unemployable. This growing group includes the young and the aged, the mentally ill and incarcerated criminals, and the growing number of women unable to take jobs because they must care for a brood of fatherless children.*

By "superfluous Americans," then, I mean human beings who have failed in a society that expects success of its citizens. Even at this late date, the United States has developed neither attitudes nor institutions capable of understanding or ameliorating the plight of unnecessary people. The successful majority continues to feel that the unemployed and the unemployable have only themselves to blame. And hence the judgment that those who have brought failure on themselves should—at the very least —be deferential and unobtrusive. While a rough-hewn Social Darwinism is no longer our official ideology, its canons remain ensconced in the public mind.

A nation that honors only achievement grows restive when attempts are made to explain the causes of failure. Despite all the exercises in sociological exoneration, the principle remains that a person be held accountable for his fate. The man who cannot find work should not have left school in a state of semi-literacy. The deserted wife and the unmarried mother ought to have thought before conceiving the children who now require social assistance. Even the mentally ill are expected to exercise just a

* Here, as elsewhere, a double standard prevails. The woman married to a job-holding husband may, honorably and without opprobrium, devote her days to child-raising and housewifely concerns. Her membership in the economy remains undisputed, due to her good fortune in choosing and holding a husband. However, women who lack resident husbands cannot claim such affiliation with the world of productive work. If they, like their more fortunate sisters, want to stay at home with their offspring, it is at society's sufferance and not as an intrinsic right.

bit more determination in trying to get a grip on themselves.

I am fully aware of the objections to my assertion concerning the economy's inability to create jobs for everyone who could or should be at work. Hence all the emphasis on the openings for nurses, secretaries, and computer programmers: we have only to glance at the advertisements in any newspaper for evidence of the need for large numbers of white-collar personnel. But I would also point out that the aggregate number of unfilled positions turns out to be far smaller than a perusal of the "Help Wanted" columns would suggest. Even if the difficulties in training unskilled laborers to use electronic equipment were overcome and all such openings were filled, only a minor fraction of the unemployed and unemployable would be absorbed into the economy.

For the critical question is how many *new* jobs the American economy can create. While employers are willing to expand their white-collar payrolls to the extent their resources allow, an enterprise aspiring to profitable operation will not add new people if it loses money by having them on its premises. (Nor do I give great weight to the theory that as more people are employed, the total demand for goods and services will be increased. The extra products such people would buy would not substantially exceed the expenditures they now make.) While it is hardly a condition on which to congratulate ourselves, honesty compels me to argue that our economy has reached a level of optimal production and profits at appreciably less than full employment.

Moreover, too much stress has been placed on the need

for education, training, and the possession of specified skills. Both employers and those already holding jobs are inclined to overemphasize the amount of schooling a person must have before he is qualified to occupy a gainful position. In reality, the most important attribute an employee must have is verbal facility: the ability to speak and act in ways customarily associated with reputable employment. Middle-class life instills in its offspring the vocabulary and demeanor required for entry into the conversational occupations. Indeed, a sensitivity to appearances permits even those with ordinary minds and limited capacities to earn quite comfortable incomes. The unemployed and underemployed Americans probably have just as much native intelligence as do those holding secure occupations. Many, in fact, have unusual talents and not unimpressive aptitudes. But, coming from backgrounds oblivious to the disciplines required by the world of work, they find no outlet for their capabilities in the productive economy. Whether the fault is theirs (for failing to cast off bad habits) or the employment system's (for its unwillingness to redraft irrelevant criteria of sociability), the fact remains that millions of Americans will continue to swell the ranks of the unemployable. Indeed, each month sees more underschooled adolescents joining this pool, and the very arrival of these new entrants counterweights the economy's efforts to assimilate people it does not need.

Furthermore, only a relatively small number are unemployed in the sense that they have been without any work at all for an extended period. The majority of superfluous Americans move in and out of the employment system, taking on temporary low-paid jobs that provide subsistence so long as they are on a payroll. I am referring, of course, to the porters and janitors, the dishwashers and domestic servants, the migrant workers, and the others we employ to do our strenuous and dirty jobs. But this kind of casual labor no longer qualifies as an honorable occupation, and those who accept it realize their marginal membership in today's economy.

Here, also, one meets the argument that there is a shortage of labor rather than a surplus. Middle-class housewives continually lament that they cannot find maids to scrub their homes and mind their children. Suburban husbands must mow their own lawns, rake their own leaves, and shovel their own driveways. Businessmen become indignant when there are no taxis waiting just when they are most needed, and commuters protest that no one scours the railroad cars into which they are herded. If skilled workers are in short supply, so are people who need have no skills at all.

There may well be a "demand" for such unskilled services. But the rates people are willing to pay for these amenities are inadequate to attract even the unemployed. Most middle-class Americans, while relatively well-off, cannot in fact afford to pay their domestic servants much more than sixty dollars per week. If a "demand" exists, it is a demand for cheap labor. At the same time, the typical middle-class family feels itself entitled to much more personal service than it is now receiving, and regards the rates it is willing to pay as eminently reasonable. Hence the admixture of perplexity and anger at the spurning of its gestures.

Each year finds fewer Americans willing to be used as cheap labor. Despite their exclusion from widespread prosperity, the expectations of the poor still parallel those of citizens in higher reaches of the economy. (This helps to explain the rising rate of burglaries and robberies in a time of prosperity.) One simply cannot be an American and receive less than three dollars for an hour's work: to earn less excludes them from most of the experiences available to the majority of the population. Sheer physical survival no longer will do. Earlier waves of immigrants, instilled with the peasant psychology, were willing to work long hours in sweatshops and servant pantries. Generations passed before such individuals even thought to protest their underpaid labor. But the peasant mentality is a thing of the past. An American may be superfluous by all economic standards, but this does not prevent him from expecting the benefits others so easily acquire. The day when the lower classes could be lectured on the need for hard work, self-control, and beginning at the bottom is long past. They know that most of their fellow citizens have undergone no such hardships, and that their own tastes and abilities differ little from those who would have them remain subordinate. Hence the inclination to take no job at all rather than labor ignobly at ill-paid employment.

The creation of new jobs, while certainly important, would solve only a small part of the problem. For the majority of the people we regard as superfluous could not earn a living in any conceivable circumstances. These individuals must, if they are to survive at all, be supported by the productive population.

America's aged constitute a good example of how the nation treats citizens who cannot make an economic contribution. Due to the longer lifespan they are experiencing if not enjoying, there are now more elderly Americans than ever before. And virtually all of them are parents of children who are themselves now well into adulthood. The attitudes and actions of these grown-up offspring reveal much about contemporary family life.

To begin with, the majority of the aged never belonged to private retirement plans to which they or their employers contributed during their working years. (Of the almost twenty million Americans over the age of sixty-five in 1967, only three million were beneficiaries of non-government pension plans.) While most now receive payments under the Social Security system, the checks they receive are depressingly meager. (In 1967 the average monthly benefit for retired workers was $82.12, or a stipend of $18.95 per week.) Hence, the elderly need subventions from local welfare agencies, and even these supplements provide little more than rent and food. (In 1968 the total median income—from all sources—for persons over sixty-five was $1,453, or $27.94 per week.)

What about their children, many of whom are now quite well-off? The answer is that only a small fraction send periodic checks to their parents. (A 1965 survey of over two million Social Security recipients revealed that fewer than eighty thousand of them received monthly cash remittances from their children.) Most younger Americans have little insight into the material condition of the aged, nor do they show any particular desire to learn the dollars-and-cents details: it is far more comfortable to assume that "the government" now provides for the economic security of the elderly. And with the tendency of young people to leave their homes and neighborhoods at an early age, the last sustained glimpse most sons and daughters have of their father was when he had a steady job and seemed relatively free of economic worries. Much easier, therefore, to conclude that one's parents have had the foresight to make plans for their non-productive years.

Very few Americans have even one parent living with them. While young adults show few compunctions about moving away from their neighborhoods, only rarely will they attempt to persuade a parent that he is wanted in the new surroundings. Most will, of course, assert that they just do not have the room to spare: even upper-middle-class Americans buy or build homes having only enough space for themselves and their own children. Quite clearly, many such families could afford an extra bedroom and bath for a widowed mother-in-law; but they prefer to devote that cash to a better location, fitting out a playroom, or installing a backyard swimming pool.

But in largest measure the repudiation of parents is related to the cultural and emotional hiatus that divides all American generations. Those raised in the postwar years have had an experience of life which gives them little in common with their parents. What is usually overlooked, however, is that this generational problem goes beyond the adult-adolescent impasse: a weakening of ties of respect, authority, and shared interests also characterizes relations between adults and their own parents. Almost as little communication and understanding exists between these sets of adults as between the two younger generations.

Hence the sequestration of a nation's grandparents. While never explicitly saying so, Americans have come to feel that the aged should be hidden from view, with the accompanying illusion that they are enjoying a life of contented relaxation. Such a belief excuses the intervals between visits, the infrequency of letters, and a lessened concern for human beings who no longer have a claim to attention.

Along with the unemployed, aged Americans find themselves unwanted. While the financial plight of the elderly deserves emphasis, their emotional isolation is even more depressing. Unable to make outright demands for respect, they must subsist on whatever tokens of affection their children choose to cast their way.

The advent of public programs—particularly retirement benefits and medical care—has served to slacken feelings of filial responsibility. Sons and daughters dream up images of congenial nursing homes and paid-up mortgages, with a benevolent government providing a modest but adequate sufficiency. The transition from financial to emotional dissociation may be grounded in logic; but, whatever its sources, it permits American parents to concentrate on themselves and their own children without having to be reminded that they, too, have mothers and fathers.

* * *

The treatment of the mentally ill reflects a similar attitude toward people whom the society could do without. A nation that takes pride in the quality of its medical care continues to shut up hundreds of thousands of mental patients in understaffed and overcrowded institutions bearing only the faintest resemblance to centers of healing. And, for all the interest expressed in psychology and psychoanalysis, serious mental impairment arouses little sympathy or attention.*

As with the aged, the nation prefers not to see the mentally ill. For too sustained a sight of those so afflicted would reveal the tenuousness of the line separating the sane from the psychotic. And just as it is supposed that public programs care for the aged, so it is assumed that state hospitals provide adequate treatment for the mentally ill. Needless to say, the interiors of these buildings seldom receive close inspection lest the illusions of adequacy be shattered.

The American people appropriate less than seven dollars per day for shelter, food, and care for the half million or so citizens confined in public institutions. The ratio of psychiatrists to patients falls short of 1-to-100; and the proportion of social workers—whose job it is to ease patients back into society—is even more disquieting. An aversion to the outlay of public funds accounts for these conditions, but a deeper underlying cause is the desire to erase all thoughts of this segment of the population. Because too attentive a concern for the mentally ill

---

* The real preoccupation, of course, is with neuroses that discommode the middle class. Not only are these more interesting for purposes of conversation, but they permit an indulgence of the self which in other circumstances would be considered unseemly.

might reveal one's own vulnerability, it is better to regard them as a breed apart and to believe that trained specialists are doing all that can be done.*

Assumptions of individual responsibility carry over into this realm also. Even educated Americans seldom mention instances of mental illness which have occurred in their families, not least because such disorders carry suggestions of weakness and failure. For all our sophistication, the puritan ethic remains strong: if a person has strength of character, he can, by an effort of will, maintain his mental integrity. Thus, euphemisms such as "nervous breakdown" continue to be used in alluding to friends and relatives unable to function in everyday life. (How many of us are willing to admit that a father or a brother has been hospitalized as a schizophrenic?) Unlike a kidney condition or even lung cancer—afflictions seen as outside the patient's control—a psychosis still connotes a moral shortcoming rather than a biochemical imbalance. Quite clearly, many Americans know better than to think and act this way. However, knowledge takes second place to fear in a society that wants everyone to exhibit the hallmarks of a productive person.

The conventional image of the American family—a mother, a father, and two or three children—requires serious revision. During the 1960s the number of families not headed by a father grew almost twice as fast as did

---

* Just about everything I have said about Americans in mental hospitals applies to the several hundred thousand citizens incarcerated in our prisons. Here, too, the public prefers not to know what happens to such individuals, nor does it display any desire to finance institutions geared to rehabilitation rather than retribution.

the number of those having two parents present. Some of these households are, of course, presided over by middle-class widows whose husbands have left them in comfortable circumstances; others include divorced women receiving regular support from their erstwhile mates. However, the majority of husbandless homes have no source of income other than public agencies. In many cases the parents never married, and the father refuses to shoulder responsibility for the children. In a greater number of instances there may once have been a husband, but death or—more likely—desertion has removed him from the scene. Sometimes such a mother will work, leaving her youngsters in the care of others or even to fend for themselves. More frequently she will simply remain at home, one of the rising proportion of women whose husbandless plight has made them the most numerous recipients of welfare funds.*

The costs of such support rise each year, but not be-

---

* To be sure, many welfare mothers could take jobs; and not a few would like nothing better than to get off the public rolls. The problem, of course, lies with their children. If a mother works, then someone must look after her youngsters while she is away. Neighborhood day-care centers have thus become a conversation-piece for those who like paper remedies for real problems. I am all in favor of such centers, if only because I think that working is good for women as well as for men. However, there must be no illusions about the costs. Decent day-care at a center now costs about $20 per child per week. Given that the typical welfare mother will take home less than $80 a week from her job, it is clear that day-care payments for two pre-school children would be far beyond her means. (Also: What about her school-age children, in the first and second grades, who are dismissed at 3:00 P.M.?) Obviously, such centers will have to be subsidized by public funds, for working mothers will be able to pay only a fraction of their true costs. Given this balance sheet, these mothers would not be self-supporting even if they did work. They would be less of a burden to society than if they were to remain wholly on welfare—but not much less.

cause of any noteworthy increases in the benefits bestowed on these fatherless households. (In 1967 a typical family—mother and children—was expected to survive on the weekly sum of $37.38.) The chief reason for these accelerating outlays lies in the rising incidence of illegitimate births.* Many unwed mothers are recruited to the welfare rolls in mid-adolescence and remain so situated for the rest of their fecund lives. And little evidence exists that lower-class marriages are improving in durability or growing less susceptible to husbandly wandering.

These millions of mothers and children have become the most visible—and most commented-upon—citizens of superfluous America. Needless to say, such mothers stand out as targets for attack: hence not only the subsistence level of welfare benefits, but also the censorious overtones to their administration. However, punishing the mothers is not enough. Even the children are treated as tainted objects who have no right to complain if their homes lack amenities. Any suggestion that the taxpaying public should support wanton women and unnecessary children in even an approximation of middle-class comfort implies that immorality would be encouraged, if not rewarded. Certainly the widespread reluctance to distin-

* In 1940 the nation's illegitimacy rate was 7.1 per 1,000 unmarried women. By 1950 it was up to 14.1, and in 1966 it stood at 23.6. More unmarried Americans are engaging in more sexual activity than ever before, and more unwanted children emerge from these unions. The threefold rise in twenty-six years is all the more striking because contraceptives are now more readily available than they were in 1940. I cannot accept the claim that there was just as much pre-marital sex a generation ago. Were this so, the illegitimacy rates of those years would surely parallel those of the present. (Nor can I believe that better reporting methods account for more than a small fraction of the statistical rise.)

guish innocent offspring from their miscreant mothers would seem to indicate that sociology has a long way to travel before it supplants puritan dogma. And even for children who were born within wedlock but whose fathers have subsequently abandoned their domestic responsibilities, too generous a level of assistance would imply that ill-advised marriages should be absolved from censure. Why, in short, must the taxpayer's purse compensate for personal indulgence?

All in all, the parsimony and penalties of welfare reflect the tendency of self-supporting citizens to pass judgment on people they deem their moral inferiors. For all their complaints over the costs of welfare, the taxpaying majority receives a substantial refund simply by being allowed to congratulate itself on its own rectitude. Probably just as much sexual misconduct occurs within the middle class as among those untutored in contraception and abortion. The sin of the poor lies in having the unwanted children that others know how to prevent. The taxpayer who prides himself on his sexual self-discipline in fact deserves credit only for his precautionary skill.*

Now America's superfluous children are beginning to pay society back, and the retribution they exact will cost us far more than would have earlier efforts at redemption. They—and their younger brothers not yet born— will roam the cities' streets terrorizing and despoiling those who made childhood a time of deprival and humiliation for them. The nation's unwillingness to share its

---

* Needless to say, sex is enjoyable. Hence the demand for lower-class abstinence, not only to discourage their costly birth rate but also to ensure that the undeserving are not enjoying themselves.

prosperity can only guarantee continued peril and disorder. Here are youngsters who grow old too early—inured in cynicism and trained in survival, persuaded by experience that this world bestows no rewards for patience or docility. Knowing that society looks upon them as unnecessary people, they will respond in the only way they know how.

To be sure, most unproductive Americans pose no direct threat to the public safety. The aged and the mentally ill, for example, do not engage in public violence or disruptive demonstrations: they seldom vote, they are difficult to organize, and only rarely does effective leadership arise from within their ranks.* Their presence constitutes only an aesthetic blemish: as citizens relegated to poverty and impotence, they are living testimony to the economy's inability to embrace people for which it has no need. Indeed, our treatment of individuals we have deemed unnecessary shows how widespread prosperity can affect the qualities of conscience and sensitivity. The fact that a society accumulates a greater ration of the good things of life does not mean that it will share that bounty with those left out or behind. The result can be just the opposite.

If most Americans now own their homes, pay taxes, and enjoy comfortable incomes, I must reiterate that success inflates the ego and good fortune heightens individuals' estimates of their qualities. Has not the nation al-

---

* Unmarried mothers, on the other hand, are beginning to develop a consciousness of their legal entitlements. Rejecting the philosophy that unsanctified sex should be punished by squalor, many are demanding incomes which will provide them with middle-class amenities. Their sense of shame has been replaced by a psychology of self-confidence and self-assertion.

ways proclaimed that prosperity and advancement go to those with superior talent and perseverance? Thus, those who have ascended conclude happily that they are built of better stuff than those for whom society has no productive place. (The puritan doctrine of predestination lives on, not due to any respect for beliefs of the past but because it continues to provide justification for contemporary arrangements.)

Moreover, the conviction of personal superiority, once the privilege of inherited wealth or self-made success, now extends through the white-collar classes and much of the wage-earning population. Tenured employment, migration to better neighborhoods, and an abundance of material possessions have implanted the taxpayer's psychology in millions who were raised in an atmosphere of insecurity and scarcity. It should come as no surprise that such citizens have little compassion to expend on people who wear all the hallmarks of indolence, wastefulness, and immorality.

These are, then, the two parts of a divided nation: Americans who have succeeded and Americans who have failed, the productive and the parasitic, those deemed necessary and those regarded as superfluous. And for the first time in the history of this or any other society the poor have become a minority. No longer have they the traditional solace of the downtrodden: the knowledge that most of the population shares their lot. It is one thing to be poor when poverty is the common condition; it is quite another when you belong to a remnant from which most of your fellow citizens have been able to escape.

Society's only wish is that the unproductive refrain from obtruding into the public vision. If they will not disappear, cannot they at least have the humility to remain well out of sight? For the spectacle of the unsuccessful rouses memories of one's own unprepossessing past and—more unsettling—the condition to which one might return. Even Americans now endowed with a modest prosperity can experience moments when they admit that they are neither as secure nor as superior as they have brought themselves to believe. At such times they realize how far they have come, and how far they could fall. Hence the need for dissociation from the world of failure. Expressions of compassion for society's deprived citizens can come easily from those in the aristocratic and professional classes, or from individuals having unusual talents or secure careers. But attitudes of fellow feeling are too hazardous a luxury for those without a net to catch them should their own social fortunes begin to falter.

Far safer to muster the self-assurance that places one on the successful side of the chasm which rends American society. The mantle of property-owner and taxpayer gives one the right to complain over the growing weight of official expenditure, to pass judgment upon those who are its recipients. Why should hard-working and tax-burdened Americans underwrite the leisure of people who contribute nothing to the commonweal? Why must an upstanding citizenry build low-rent housing that will soon become gang-infested slums or raise air-conditioned schools for children who are probably unteachable? To ask an American electorate to invest in such projects on any but the most token scale is fruitless.

Also, underlying the accusations of extravagance and

inefficiency is the fear that improvement of the condition of the unproductive might narrow—or even close—the divide now separating the two Americas. For the poor are no longer asking for a pittance. An annual "guaranteed family income" of $3,500 or even $4,000 will no longer satisfy any but the vestiges of our rural peasantry. Even an aged couple or a woman with several children now expects a standard of life which requires a yearly income of at least $8,000. But such a figure would place our unproductive members on a parity with Americans who work a full week to earn such wages and who must provide the taxes to support the superfluous. Yet if it is no longer possible to instill humility in the poor and unproductive, it is equally impossible to persuade the rest of us to be more generous. General prosperity creates new expectations, even among those denied a share of its emoluments. Thus, an era that bestows affluence on the majority of a population witnesses tensions of a sort seldom seen when most citizens know only privation. America is in the midst of a struggle between two identifiable classes. The Marxian model of bourgeoisie-versus-proletariat may no longer apply: but the confrontation is real and its peaceful resolution remains unlikely.

One fact is clear: there can be no return to an economy wherein unproductive individuals were absorbed into the bosom of the family and the circle of the community. American democracy has widened the horizons of untold millions. As a consequence, it deals sternly with those who fail to pass the tests of productive contribution.

5: *Civil War*

DURING THE 1930s in New York City, the black-white boundary ran along Morningside Avenue. My family lived on 123rd Street, just on the west—the white—side of that frontier. East of Morningside one was in Harlem. Yet only whites crossed this line. Apart from some domestic servants and an occasional delivery boy, entire days might go by without a black face appearing in adjacent white neighborhoods. On the other hand, those of us who were white never regarded Morningside Avenue as a barrier. We felt entirely free to wander into Harlem at any hour of the day or night, feeling secure that we would be neither accosted nor attacked. These were Depression years, and Harlem was by all odds the poorest section of the city. It could well have been dangerous territory for any white trespasser. Nevertheless, it was entirely safe.

The reason, of course, was that the blacks knew their place. Not only did they avoid white territory; they also realized that they must not approach whites who happened to stroll through their slum. Fear of the police obviously helped maintain this submission; for in those days Harlem's station houses were even less attentive to due processes of law than they are now. A far more effective control, however, lay in the tacit understanding that members of America's subordinate races simply did not touch or threaten their betters. This is by no means to suggest that black Americans were happy with their condition. Their mood was rather one of resignation; any impulse to protest fell victim to the presence of white domination within the black consciousness.

Before World War II, America's black population constituted neither a threat nor a problem for the white nation. The black minority subsisted under effective control in the rural South and also in the Northern slums, where intimidation and oppression were usually implicit but nonetheless real. Moreover, little attention was paid to the condition of black Americans. It was assumed, for example, that a docile pool of black labor would always be available for the arduous and unskilled services required by white society. No thoughts were raised concerning where housemaids or porters went or what they did after their working hours. Black America remained unobtrusive, apparently uncomplaining, and virtually invisible to white eyes.

These were placid years for white Americans. No serious civil-rights movement or organized protests arose to upset white sensibilities. No talk of black power was

97

heard, and only the barest whispers of equalitarian aspirations could be detected. Aware of the totality of their
thralldom, black Americans simply saw no prospect for
improving their bleak experience of life. They knew that
they were marginal members of the nation, and realized
that white America looked upon them as an awkward ap-
pendage, not quite human in major respects, and to be
consigned to the end of the queue when scarce commodities were apportioned.

The most significant change for the black man has
been not in his condition relative to white America, but
rather in his perception of himself. Black Americans now
feel entitled to more from the society that surrounds
them. This transformation began during the Second
World War, when, for the first time, black Americans
were actually courted by the white society. A labor shortage in private industry forced employers to offer jobs to
workers who would previously have been excluded from
consideration. Even the most exploited of domestic servants discovered that they, too, could exact better wages
and working conditions. A human being's discovery that
he is needed and wanted can be a catalyzing experience,
forging a new conception of his own identity and accelerating the desire for even greater recognition. Once a
society has told men and women that it cannot function
without their participation, they will not willingly revert
to less favorable conceptions of themselves when the
crisis has passed.

Thus, the notions of civil rights and racial integration,
the ideas of social equality and black power, had their
origins in the wartime years. A new black mind was

forged by events that had been neither planned nor anticipated. For even so brief a sojourn in the sun as the wartime years afforded was sufficient to introduce black Americans to incomes, occupations, and expectations that had hitherto been the exclusive preserve of white citizens.

The protests of the postwar generation signified an end to an acceptance of the half-slave, half-free status that had persisted for almost a century following the Civil War. Now blacks mounted new responses to displays of injustice. Now the white nation encountered arrogance and anger for which it was not prepared.

The unintended effect of World War II was thus to destroy the controls that had given race relations a placid appearance. Just as the war transformed the white population, instilling in average people new aspirations, so black Americans found reason to believe that their history could take a new turning. Blacks showed themselves willing to jeopardize their lives and livelihoods as never before. The risks of arrest and imprisonment and bodily harm are now accepted, as is even the eventuality of death.

But if the psychology of black America has altered, the material reality of black life has changed only at the margin. By all comparative measures, the nation's black citizens still find themselves confined to the status they knew a generation ago: in terms of the jobs they manage to obtain, the quality of education their children receive, the habitations in which they must live, and their over-all level of health and well-being. Such amelioration as has occurred has been part of the general escalation in the living standard of the entire society. Today's blacks may be better off than were those of a generation ago, but the test is whether the gap between the races shows signs of diminishing. And this has not occurred.

In other words, for all the social and material gains that some blacks have experienced, no white man has been supplanted in the process. Given the existence of many talented and imaginative blacks and many whites having only marginal abilities, any meaningful moves toward racial equality would necessarily entail the demotion of several million white citizens so that more capable blacks could take their places. The fact that such transpositions have not occurred has not gone unobserved by black Americans.*

Thus, by all significant indices, America's blacks remain clustered at the bottom of the nation's social structure. Moreover, for all the protests and the inflation of black expectations, time will bring little noteworthy progress toward a racial parity. Indeed, all signs now point to a hardening of racial lines, and there is reason to believe that the relative condition of the black race will actually worsen over the coming decades.

---

* To be sure, a disproportionate number of blacks have recently been appointed to judgeships, admitted to top-ranking colleges, and given promotions in the armed services. And it must obviously follow that if such scarce positions are given to blacks, then some white candidates will be passed over. But there is no shortage of alternative rewards for the whites who are deprived of prizes due to the symbolic admission of a number of blacks. Certainly the white youth who finds that "his" place at Harvard has been taken by a black applicant need not look forward to a lifetime of unskilled labor: he will have to settle for Cornell. There are enough honorable opportunities for whites of even middling talent so that the promotion of a few blacks to what were once white echelons does not result in any perceptible sacrifice for the white community.

A candid analysis of the social character of America's black population compels such a forecast. It is certainly true that some hundreds of thousands of blacks have come to share incomes and occupations once open only to whites, but this fact diminishes in significance when set against the accelerating growth of a vast black under-population. Listing statistics on the numbers of blacks admitted to universities or given corporate white-collar jobs only deflects attention from those beyond the reach of education or employment. The critical figures are far more elementary: black birth rates and black patterns of migration give the real picture of the racial future.

For a child conceived tonight will be the adolescent of tomorrow and the adult of the day after. The tenant farmer currently subsisting in rural Mississippi will soon move to New Orleans and thence to Chicago. The growing bulk of black America consists not of a few hundred thousand who have attained middle-class status but rather the millions of marginal men, women, and children for whom white society has neither need nor sympathy. These black Americans will make their presence felt, no matter what the opinion or reaction of white America turns out to be.

The Southern economy has declared that it no longer needs its black minority. Blacks have been deemed superfluous people for whom fewer and fewer productive jobs will be available each year. Not only have the mechanization of agriculture and the consolidation of farming rendered black labor redundant, but the large cities of the South hold out little promise of honorable employment for those forced off the land. The unwritten economic code of the region is clear: whatever new jobs may be created must first be offered to the white citizenry. The South has more than enough underemployed whites to take over the workbenches of new factories, the desks of new offices, and the counters of new shopping centers. Blacks are invited into the labor force only when the pool of available whites is depleted. Better than anyone, the Southern black understands the rules of this game. He realizes he will have to bide his time at the tail end of the "Help Wanted" lines, and he has seen all too many of those signs taken down before his name was called. So he travels North.

Buses and trains have been pulling into Chicago, Detroit, Cleveland, Los Angeles, New York, and Philadelphia every day and night for a generation, disgorging exiles from Alabama, Mississippi, Louisiana, and South Carolina. Sometimes a father comes alone, to search for a job and a place to live, intending to send for his family later on. Not infrequently the arrival will be a weary mother with a brood of young children, coming to find the husband who has departed some months earlier and whose subsequent silence casts doubts on his future family role.

But the North, like the South, has no real need for this flood of strangers.* Few meaningful jobs can be created for these migrants, and they must squeeze themselves into the already overcrowded tenements that white map-

* This, of course, constitutes the critical difference between this and earlier migrations. Throughout the nineteenth century there was a continual demand for uneducated and unskilled labor, and every white immigrant off the boat—including women and children—could find a job of some sort without effort or embarrassment.

makers designate as their territory. But at least no one need suffer malnutrition in the North. Welfare departments provide subsistence for unemployable women and children, and in the interstices of urban life men can find the small pickings of odd jobs and petty crime. The real scarcity lies in steady and moderately remunerative employment for black men, and even those who manage to get and hold jobs for sustained periods find few prospects for advancement. The conventional precept that intelligence and industry will be rewarded with promotion and affluence applies only to those born with white skins. Blacks realize that, no matter how hard they may work, they will still remain society's porters and janitors and dishwashers. If one requisite for promotion is the ability to make a favorable impression on others, the mere possession of a black exterior precludes being taken wholly seriously. Excluded from traditional rewards and incentives, millions of black men move out of the system. Given similar prospects for success, the same proportion of whites would end up on urban streetcorners.

The facts of ghetto life compound this condition. These enclaves are created and sustained not by their actual residents but by whites who live elsewhere. Simply by denying black fellow citizens freedom of housing, white America stakes out the residual areas where blacks may live. To be sure, a few blacks do manage to break out of these confines (and others claim that they could move, but remain in the ghetto by choice). However, the majority, and especially the new arrivals, must make their homes in the slums. The ghetto's boundaries are always expanding as a few more blacks move into proximate streets, thereby accelerating the exodus of remaining whites. But every better-off black knows the difficulty of leapfrogging into white neighborhoods: the humiliations he will encounter in his search for a home in such off-limits territory, and the risks he and his family will endure if he tries to settle among inhospitable household-ers. For this reason alone much of the black middle class continues to live in the ghetto.

Department stores and restaurants, hospitals and universities, municipal offices and police stations, even airplanes and interstate highways are all white estates. Indeed, the entire country—apart from its ghettoes—is white property where non-whites know they have no license to tarry after they have completed the approved errands that brought them there.*

The black ghetto may well be a community; indeed, it may warrant that designation far more than most white neighborhoods. Yet, for all the shared experience and camaraderie of its residents, the ghetto also exhibits a greater measure of anarchy than any other region of American society. Crime, violence, and the sheer risk to life and limb are of epidemic proportions. (The odds that a resident will suffer physical assault are 130 times greater in a black slum than in a white middle-class suburb.) The police provide protection at only minimal levels; danger lurks on the streets and in the tenements,

* The United States does not—as yet—have a formal "pass" system. However, whites invariably assume that anyone who possesses a black face ought to explain his presence. "What are *you* doing here?" is the continual question in white minds, and the very look he is given tells the black man that such a question is being raised. In effect, a black skin is a "non-pass," a negative credential that automatically casts doubt on its holder's right to enter off-limits territory.

for blacks have no compunctions about preying on their fellow blacks.* Quite clearly, the ghetto is no fit place to raise children. Any hope that parents may have of exerting influence over their children suffers defeat once their youngsters reach the streets. Schoolyards and sidewalks become recruiting grounds for gangs, and youthful friends as often as not lead one another into temptations that take a mortal toll before adolescence has ended. The

---

* It is no paradox that black citizens complain about *both* the lack of police protection and the incidence of police brutality. Most crime is intra-racial: that is to say, the majority of crimes committed by black criminals are perpetrated against members of their own race. And this is the chief reason why the police show less concern when responding to calls in the ghetto. For the typical policeman cannot bring himself to believe that the criminal injuries suffered by black citizens deserve the attention accorded to those inflicted on whites. This double standard results in inadequate police protection for the residents of black slums.

At the same time, police efforts to preserve order are based on shotgun methods and racial stereotypes. Hardly a black American of any class has not experienced discourtesy—or worse—at police hands. For most policemen make no attempt to distinguish between law-abiding blacks and those who may be presumptive criminals. Hence all blacks are treated in the same way: all are regarded either as having committed a crime or as likely to be embarked on one. If the black demand is for more police protection—which means more police patrolling the ghetto—it is also for policemen who treat black citizens with some semblance of human respect.

The answer, however, is not simply recruiting more black policemen to urban forces and then assigning them to ghetto duty. For so long as black policemen depend for their promotions and preferment on white superiors, they will simply mirror the behavior of their white colleagues and supervisors. Indeed, it is a ghetto truism that black police can be even more vicious and vindictive toward members of their own race. The only "solution" would be to permit ghetto areas to recruit and control their own police forces, including choice of commanders and supervision of procedures. But there is little prospect of white city councils and state legislatures permitting such a move. Quite clearly, white lawmakers feel that black citizens lack the capacity for handling so critical a responsibility. (Let me add, finally, that the election of black mayors will not be much help. For mayors are remarkably powerless when it comes to controlling the police.)

street forms the focus of life, and exacts its price: heroin addiction, arrest and imprisonment, prostitution, or simply the lackluster life of semi-literacy and sporadic employment. Boys have police records before their fifteenth birthday; girls become pregnant before turning sixteen. (This is not, of course, a "racial pathology"; white Americans of all classes engage in self-destructive behavior. But far fewer whites are raised in ghettoes, and thus their chances of prison or pregnancy are lower.)

And in these pregnancies lies the future of black America. Half the black births in Northern cities occur out of wedlock, a figure unlikely to undergo substantial reduction during the next several decades. Moral censure, or even the threat of lessened welfare payments, will not alter the ghetto's sexual habits. For these progenitive adolescents live in a world where puritanical or even precautionary morality has little relevance. To expect such boys and girls to exhibit self-restraint or to adhere to a code created by an alien and uncaring society is self-deception. Those who preoccupy themselves with the immorality and irresponsibility found in slum society would do well to turn their attention to the new generations of youngsters being spawned in our ghettoes this very moment. These infants will be adolescents fifteen years hence and potential criminals, terrorists, and unemployed a decade thereafter. Having come into the world unwanted by their parents and unneeded by society, they stand only the slightest chance of knowing love or encouragement or even recognition of their humanity. In the process of creation right now are rioters and rapists, murderers and marauders, who will despoil society's landscape before this century has run its course.

This underpopulation dominates the black birth rate and by sheer power of numbers decelerates all efforts at racial amelioration. Prior to 1970 it was customary to refer to blacks as comprising one-tenth of the American nation. However, white America would be well advised to pay closer heed to the official statistics. Of the infants now being born, blacks account not for one in ten but closer to one in six. Black Americans will always be a minority; but as the white birth rate declines, that minority will start to approach 20 or perhaps 25 percent of the population.

The time has come for some unwelcome candor: to admit that white America does not want to deploy its resources toward redeeming the black citizenry. Any meaningful amelioration of black America's condition would require money and effort, personnel and priorities—indeed, moral and emotional commitments—that the white society simply will not muster. If the merest hope of survival were to be granted to millions of black children, they would have to have care and attention costing many times what even the most prosperous of suburbs give to their own sons and daughters. Such a mission of rehabilitation would call for a virtual army of nursery-school teachers, public health nurses, building inspectors, rat exterminators, probation officers, welfare workers, and—not least important—policemen willing and able to render effective service in the black ghettoes.*

---

* Few whites show any enthusiasm for entering these occupations, much less for working in ghetto areas. Even though money is frequently available for hiring more teachers, nurses, and caseworkers, slum schools and hospitals remain inadequately staffed. Many of these

However, white America, which pays most of the country's taxes and elects all save a handful of its lawmakers, cannot be stirred beyond a conversational concern. Although the nation may seem preoccupied with racial vicissitudes, its principal output has been little more than a series of paper programs and endless conferences, commissions, and committees. (Indeed, simply talking about "race" and "poverty" earns comfortable incomes for no small number of publishers, publicists, and social scientists.) And while white America debates the wisdom of spending another billion dollars on yet another public project, the condition of the black under-population continues to worsen. The much publicized pre-school centers, job-training agencies, and birth-control clinics reach only a fraction of those in need of such assistance. And when we take into account the annual arrival of new infants and in-migrants, the services which are available actually end up aiding an even smaller segment of our urban ghettoes than they did the year before.

Those who write reports almost invariably conclude their remarks with the word "massive." They tell us that programs and appropriations must be "massive" if slums

---

positions could be filled by ghetto residents (the amount of training necessary for most such jobs has been vastly overemphasized). Even so, there are not nearly enough black dentists or lawyers or psychiatrists to serve the slum populations, nor will there be for several decades. And while a few young professionals may commit themselves to terms of ghetto service, the number of volunteers will be far too small to achieve anything more than token amelioration. If the condition of black America is to undergo serious improvement, it must have substantially superior social and human services, not all of which can be provided by black personnel and only a fraction of which can be financed by black dollars.

are to be rehabilitated, schools reformed, and the employment system restructured. This is true, but America's racial situation has reached the point where deploying a major portion of the nation's resources would only just begin to alter prevailing imbalances. However, the only "massive" endeavor will be the continued use of that word. White taxpayers have no disposition to sacrifice their personal prosperity, especially to assist blacks— and no evidence can be produced to show that this attitude can or will be transformed by new information, exhortations, or appeals.

Black Americans realize this. Few have any illusions about white America's readiness to underwrite anything more than research and conferences. No one should be surprised at the more open displays of black resentment and rage. At the same time, it would be a mistake to attribute these stirrings to disillusionment over unfilled promises. It is certainly true that for almost two decades official pronouncements have appeared to hold out prospects for substantial amelioration. Supreme Court decisions, Presidential directives, and acts of Congress have declared that school segregation, housing discrimination, and poverty itself would be brought to an end. These pledges, impressive on paper, may well have raised some black expectations; their meager implementation certainly fueled black cynicism. But three centuries of experience have inured black Americans to the failure of white promises, even those issued by the most authoritative of agencies. Black discontent, therefore, does not arise from inadequate delivery on official assurances. Rather its source lies in the contrasting conditions of life known by the two races. That contrast, so evident to blacks, is the chief wellspring of anger. And that mood would still be present even had government been less grandiose in its commitments to racial reform.

Violence will mark relations between the races. Whites will live in increasing fear of depredations against their persons and property. And the grim overtones of race will exacerbate white fears: for being accosted by a black carries an added quotient of terror compared with robbery by a member of one's own race. The condition of the black population is such that the number entering its criminal class—particularly adolescents and young adults—rises each year. Consider the black infants born this morning: there is no reason to believe that the lives most of them will know in the next sixteen years will deter them from committing acts of violence. No special prescience is needed to forecast the treatment they will receive from their birth through adolescence, so their subsequent behavior should hardly surprise us. Moreover, black animosities now express themselves more openly, and each criminal act against a white yields not only its material dividend but also the pleasure of exacting some small revenge for centuries of racial wrongs. Even though black criminal violence is not part of any organized strategy, the fears aroused by such activity are as real as those stirred by purposive demonstrations.

The number of attempts to sabotage the mechanisms of government and society will grow. In addition to peaceful demonstrations such as marches and picketing, the country will be confronted by not-so-peaceful efforts at blocking traffic, impeding business, and disrupting white America's normal routines. Millions of black Americans have no incentive to identify with these institutions, and hence no compunctions about undermining their functioning. On occasion these disruptions will simply be mischievous: sending in false fire alarms, tying up telephone lines, closing off entrances to buildings, jamming roads at rush hours. However, the time will come when the malice will outweigh the mischief, often involving serious destruction: dynamiting of bridges and water mains, firing of buildings, assassination of public officials and private luminaries.

And of course there will be occasional rampages, for which the raw ingredients are always available. Start with a spring or summer day when cramped apartments force ghetto residents onto the streets, combine with a rumor of police brutality, add the thunderclap of a nearby store-window shattering to the pavement. It requires no more than this to release energies pent up by a lifetime of frustration. However, these exercises in violence occur only within the confines of the slums, and most participants content themselves with a little looting. No sorties into white territory follow, if only because anyone who might attempt such an expedition knows he would be cut off, surrounded, and decimated once he entered enemy ground. (White householders who arm themselves against a black invasion of their suburban homes underestimate black intelligence.) Ghetto rampages cannot be called "race riots," at least not in the traditional understanding of that term, for they do not involve physical confrontations between one race and another. They are, rather, excursions in community vandalism having at least some insurrectionary overtones, for the chief targets are alien-owned property inside the ghetto.

Not all violence involves assaults on persons or property. While human relationships can range from amiable to abrasive, most people become habituated to at least the appearance of civility. Therefore, when friction starts, those unprepared begin to find everyday life a more jarring experience. Until very recently white Americans could take it for granted that their relations with blacks would move according to form. Blacks wore the appropriate mask in the white man's presence, smiling or deferential as the occasion warranted. This demeanor was itself evidence that whites were in control: the capacity to exact an expected countenance is an impressive display of power. But black eyes no longer smile so readily. More and more blacks glare straight back, their expressions reflecting insolence and contempt. This black gaze unsettles white sensibilities, undermining all traditional feelings of command. (To white liberals it is disturbing in a special way—individuals who profess sympathy for the black cause feel they should be exempted from such scornful glances.) The ways people look at, pass by, or brush against one another always imply their respective standings. The readiness of blacks to say—with their eyes, their dress, their intonations—that they will no longer wear their old masks is a gauntlet thrown at white faces. Given the accustomed conventions, it is an act of violence.

For all the erosion of black deference, expressions of black power are sporadic. The consciousness of more than twenty million people does not change overnight. Nevertheless, the emergence of black pride has been surprisingly sudden, and for this reason real mobilization may occur much sooner than current disorganization would suggest. But black Americans have yet to mount the kind of rebellion typical of a people victimized by alien oppressors. It is noteworthy—at least with the close of the 1960s—how few acts of organized terror have been staged by blacks.

Only a dozen or so young, committed men and women in any slum of several hundred thousand are required for a series of symbolic acts. Why, for example, have no white policemen been found in ghetto alleys or tenement hallways, their throats slit ear to ear? (Of course, neighbors must be willing to shield the perpetrators, risking arrest, interrogation, and imprisonment.) This sort of violence prevailed in Europe throughout the German occupation, in Palestine during the British mandate, and in Algeria prior to the French withdrawal. But it has yet to happen in New York's Harlem and Bedford-Stuyvesant or Chicago's South and West Sides. Moreover, blacks in the South have had endless opportunities to fire shots at white sheriffs patrolling rural roads. The failure of black America to produce even a score of men willing to display such resistance shows how strong are the controls which have held that race submissive for so long. Yet, given the contemporary ferment, the occurrence of symbolic terrorism becomes more and more likely. The very laws of chance—the emergence of twenty-five guerrilla warriors from among twenty-five million—hurtle in this direction.

White America's responses can easily be predicted. Unwilling to undergo either the emotional adjustments or material sacrifices necessary to correct racial inequities, whites will adhere to less costly alternatives: retreat, resistance, repression.

Indeed, the white majority has already committed itself to a course whose effect, if not intention, will be to frustrate the most pressing of black aspirations. White wealth, white votes, plus the sheer preponderance of white numbers, will be used to preserve the style of life white Americans have won for themselves in recent decades. The white population has nothing to gain and everything to lose by any significant alteration of the lines now separating the races. For if a single word characterizes white attitudes, it is *fear*.

But how can a black minority, a small and impoverished segment of a huge society, arouse such anxiety in 180 million hearts and minds? The threat, of course, lies not so much in the power blacks can deploy as in the vulnerability of whites when faced with the prospect of black proximity. Material prosperity, heightened status, enhanced schooling, increased articulateness—none of these advances have succeeded in dispelling white fears of the black presence. Indeed, the spread of affluence and education actually serve to exacerbate this disquiet. Individuals who have experienced recent elevations in status are the most easily frightened.

Nightmares of racial inundation alternate with prayerful daydreams of blacks voluntarily reverting to earlier roles. Why don't *they* remain in their own parts of town instead of trying to push into places where they are not wanted? Why can't *they* send their children to the schools in their own neighborhoods rather than unsettle the entire system with demands for altering traditional boundaries? Why don't *they* work their own way up the economic ladder instead of insisting upon preferential consideration? Why don't *they* teach their sons and daughters respect for law, order, and authority? Underlying such meditations is the hope that they will cease their demands and return to a status and psychology less threatening to white sensibilities.

While these hopes linger in most white hearts, styles of expression differ. Conservatives air their views with little diffidence. Those professing a greater liberality must ponder such thoughts in silence, for commitments to equality are now accompanied by fears of violence. Hence, the liberal wants blacks to stay in their ghettoes, with the hope that they will be happy there. The conservative also favors such sequestration, but does not really care whether the blacks are happy in the ghetto or anywhere else.

Hence the end of all illusions that black Americans may have harbored about an alliance with white liberalism. While liberals may extend verbal sympathy on appropriate occasions, they continue their exodus to the suburbs or the more secure portions of the city, they place their children in private schools, and they ask fewer questions about the ways the police guard them from presumptive criminals. Apart from rhetoric ("massive expenditures" for rehabilitation of the ghettoes, "crash programs" of job training), little distinguishes the behavior of white liberals from that of their conservative neighbors. The latter express their obduracy and animosities with a candor that may be frightening but at least has the virtue of frankness.

The scenario is all too familiar. A black couple enters a white neighborhood on a Sunday afternoon to inquire about purchasing a house or renting an apartment. This in itself is enough to arouse tremors, for such visitors are seen as heralds of an invasion. Every map of metropolitan America shows territory lost to the blacks: once one is let in, the rest will follow. Admit a black teacher or even a physician or engineer, and on his heels will arrive unwed mothers, drug addicts, and adolescent gangs. To be sure, some white householders profess their desire to have a black family on their block and one or two well-scrubbed and well-mannered black youngsters in their own children's classrooms. Tokens of this sort can be redeemed at the bank of conscience with compounded interest. ("Well, we have one four doors down from us." "My daughter has one in her class.") Yet second thoughts often follow, for what begins as a magnanimous gesture can become an aperture through which a flood will rush. This is why the United States has no "integrated" neighborhoods to speak of, only "changing" ones.

Thus the tide moves on, sometimes slowly but always inexorably. Areas once immaculately white turn speckled and then black. The rear guard eventually flees, abandoning homes and schools in rapid disarray. But fewer and fewer hiding places remain. Having retreated to the city's outer reaches or into the adjacent suburbs,

resettled homeowners may discover specks beginning to
blemish the terrain they thought would be secure. Why
this fear of black contagion? Part of the reason lies in
attempts by white citizens to safeguard their modest material fortunes. A majority of Americans now own their
own homes, or at least bear responsibility for discharging
an unpaid mortgage. The graduation of so many to the
rank of homeowner has been widely applauded, for it
was thought that attainment of this status would enhance
identity and personal independence. Yet the burdens of
ownership can be emotional as well as financial: not only
does a change in a neighborhood's racial composition
threaten a lifetime's investment, but anxieties begin to
take their toll well before the day of crisis actually arrives. Current preoccupations over status, economic loss,
and physical safety create and exacerbate racial antago-
nisms to a far greater degree than prevailed when people
lacked so proprietary an interest in their homes.

The majority of black Americans are poor: the poorest Americans are black, and even the most prosperous
blacks are still poorer than great numbers of whites. If all
25 million black Americans were to be ranked by their
incomes, every single individual on that list would have
less money than his white counterpart of parallel ranking. Thus, the black who stands 17,376,289th among the
25 million blacks has a lower income than the white man
standing 128,584,539th among the 184 million whites.

The implications in these figures should be apparent.
Racial integration of American neighborhoods would
have to be class integration as well. If 50 blacks moved
into any neighborhood now containing 370 whites,

every one of those blacks would be poorer than at least some of the whites, and a majority of them would be poorer than any of their white neighbors.

Very few Americans want to live among individuals of a class lower than their own. The disappearance of traditional tokens of status has caused a person's residence to become a critical measure of his social standing. The casual question "Where do you live?" seeks not only information about a person's tastes but also some approximation of his class ranking. Where you live signals not only what you can afford but also whether you are headed up, down, or marking time. To reside in a successful neighborhood is a symbol of personal success; to remain in one that is failing conveys a less joyous message. Few of us wish to risk an unfavorable judgment. Those who live amid inferior classes jeopardize the image they present to employers and associates whose favor they may require.

The very presence of poor people—especially poor blacks—easily unsettles middle-class sensibilities. Were neighborhoods to contain a mixture of races and classes, middle-class individuals would find themselves living amid conditions they now manage to avoid. The poor reside in more crowded circumstances, often with several families inhabiting a single-family dwelling. (For this reason, and because money is unavailable for other activities, they also spend more time on the sidewalks and streetcorners.) The poor have more fatherless families, more free-wheeling children, and seem less committed to civil proprieties. And the poorer an area, the greater the incidence of drunkenness and drug addiction and violence both on and off the streets. Personal property and bodily safety are more vulnerable to depredations in less prosperous settings, and police seem to feel that the poor deserve less protection or attention than do better-off citizens.

As blacks arrive in a district and whites depart, such territory becomes more susceptible to burglary and assault. Once even a few blacks begin to reside in an area, their faces become part of the local landscape and members of their race who are not residents find it easier to make criminal forays into that zone. (A black face tends to rouse suspicions in all-white terrain, even when its bearer is on the most respectable of errands.) Given this, middle-class Americans prefer to escape to neighborhoods that are clean and secure. Moreover, the middle class has become quite fastidious when confronted by violence: men who wear white collars and work at sedentary jobs have had little experience of fighting, and for them the prospect of being mugged may be far more terrifying than for those who live and work in less prepossessing surroundings.

This condition of mind precludes any possibility of establishing interclass—and certainly interracial—neighborhoods. In the past, mixed neighborhoods were not totally unknown: in small towns and parts of large cities, private houses and tenements often stood side by side. But in those generations social controls were effective; the poor understood their place, and their presence held no threat to citizens of higher station. Such residential patterns were possible because each neighbor appreciated where he ranked in the community, and he was aware that certain behavior would be deemed presumptuous for one of his income. But with the erosion of these controls, interclass living has become too great a gamble for the classes that have most to lose by such integration.*

And there are, of course, the children. A democracy's parents must fight to guarantee the success of their children just as the animals of the jungle struggle to protect their young. Offspring of a democracy arrive in the world with neither inherited wealth nor the promise of subsequent prosperity. If they are to pass the tests and secure the credentials that society requires of those who inhabit its upper reaches, then parental assistance is necessary in the formative years.

Hence the attempts to bestow on the children the advantages they will need in the competitions to come. Anxious and often obsessive attention becomes focused on the right school, the right college, the right course of study, the right career. In the upper middle classes only an irresponsible handful fails to attend parents' meetings. They come not so much to check up on the school and

* Residential and educational integration has ceased to be either an issue or an aspiration for many blacks. For some, the prospect of living among whites holds no real attraction: hence the growing preference for a separate community and culture. Others have concluded that integrated schools and neighborhoods are no longer possible: the black population is too large, too poor, and too concentrated to be dispersed throughout white America. Nevertheless, integration remains an important—and fearsome—symbol for white Americans. Hence the referenda defeating open-housing statutes, the legislation against busing, and all the frantic efforts to keep blacks off their blocks and out of their children's classrooms. Even blacks who no longer desire integration see such measures as continuing evidence of white rejection and white predisposition to stigmatize all blacks with the real or imagined sins of a few. In short, the reactions to proposals for integration tell us more about the attitudes and anxieties of white America than about the ambitions of black citizens.

its teachers—although that motive is often present—as to pledge their allegiance to an institution that promises to ensure their children's ascent to a more elevated status.

A democracy's children must be taught to avoid improper associations if they are to emerge as successful adults in a competitive society. But such an education can only be achieved in a good school in a good neighborhood—a white middle-class school in a white middle-class neighborhood.

Unless properly shielded from injurious influences, every boy and girl is a candidate for the nether-world of failures. (For one's offspring to have failed, moreover, becomes a commentary on the parents' ability to carry out the enterprise of child-rearing.) Adults who have made modest progress toward new plateaus know from their own upbringing the consequences of misguided associations. They realize how slum environments and inferior schools can nullify a youngster's prospects. Hence the frantic effort of white Americans to insulate their sons and daughters from the presence of subordinate classes. The fear is of contagion; the disease is failure.

Because of the separation of races and classes, a generation of white children has been raised overhearing endless discussions concerning the gap that divides black from white and poor from prosperous. Most of these children have been reared in white neighborhoods and attended white schools, facts that further instill in them the idea that races belong apart. Even if their parents refrain from lecturing them on the results of admitting blacks to their schools and neighborhoods, white boys and girls overhear enough to become convinced that such incursions would have baneful consequences. The racial attitudes of today's children—tomorrow's adults—become ingrained at an early age; outlooks implanted during these years may not be extirpated after the beginning of adulthood.

There is little reason, then, to believe that oncoming generations of white Americans will display more tolerance than did their parents. For all the espousals of human equality and racial brotherhood heard from adolescents and young adults, they will in time assume responsibilities that will preclude the fulfillment of these vows. They, like their elders before them, will become burdened with families, mortgages, and careers. The comforts and pleasures of possessions will make them less than eager to undergo sacrifices for the sake of others; and anxieties over the advancement of their own offspring will send them to the safety of all-white suburbs. Given the opportunities they will grasp and the lives they will lead, it is impossible to see how tomorrow's adult generation will differ from today's. The proximity of contaminating races and classes would certainly threaten their status and security no less than it has their parents'. And the conversations their children will overhear may well be marked by bitterness and fear.

Of course, conditions can change. But change can take the direction of increasing tension, rising animosity, and exacerbated conflict. Anyone who argues that tomorrow's Americans will act more salubriously in matters of race and class must show that the future will somehow exempt these individuals from the strains and anxieties which attend child-raising, career-building, and competition for social success. If people are to be more relaxed about their surroundings and less preoccupied with their personal status and safety, then the structure and psychology of the nation will have to undergo deep-seated changes. Otherwise the growth of racial amity will remain a wishful forecast rather than a reality.

The white retreat will be accompanied by efforts at resistance and repression. As criminal violence, riots, and guerrilla activity become more frequent, white Americans will seek to maintain order by force. Police will be granted an even wider latitude in their enforcement procedures and will not have to answer for their methods. New centers of incarceration will be built, new weaponry invented and distributed to accommodate the assumption that every black man between the ages of fifteen and thirty-five may be considered a presumptive criminal. No explanation will need to be given for detaining citizens of such race and age, for in the eyes of white society the statistical probabilities demonstrate that enough individuals in these categories will sooner or later run afoul of the law or jeopardize public order. These assumptions will inflict unjust punishments on many innocent black individuals simply because they are members of a group having an above-average record of criminal convictions. But the burden will be placed on each black man to prove his innocence of any wrongdoing, past, present, or future. And his consignment to jail, with or without much attention to the evidence, will be regarded as the removal of one more miscreant from society's streets.

And having concluded that official agencies can no

longer guarantee protection, more and more citizens of both races will purchase guns. Women's purses, executives' attaché cases, and automobiles' glove compartments will hold such weapons, as will the drawers of bedside tables in countless homes across the country. As more people own guns, the use of firearms will inevitably increase, accompanied by the plea of "self-defense." Judges and juries will find themselves under growing pressure to render verdicts of "justifiable homicide," particularly in cases where white householders take the lives of black intruders.

Whether construed as a state of siege or a condition of civil war, strains between the races will suffuse all aspects of the nation's life. The resentments harbored by black Americans have yet to erupt in full expression; the generation of young blacks now emerging will mount demands that white America cannot possibly accommodate; and society's conventional instruments of amelioration will prove both inadequate and irrelevant as both races react in an atmosphere of tension and fright.

What scares and frustrates white Americans most, however, is their knowledge that racial arrangements are no longer under control. After ten generations of submission, blacks now display anger and arrogance that white society can neither command nor understand. Thus, black behavior must be seen as an exercise of power—psychological and physical as well as political— which American society never anticipated. The riots, robberies, and assaults, even the modes of dress and contemptuous stares with which blacks meet white glances, are all symbols of racial uprising. As much a mood as a

movement, as much guerrilla war as partisan maneuver-
ing, black power has already achieved its greatest victory: the demoralization of white society. The awareness
that blacks can no longer be ruled by hitherto effective
controls has undermined white self-confidence. Repression will surely follow. But the use of force will only be a
frantic quest for protection and survival by a people
whose morale has been shattered by the surfacing of an
inequality that was always inherent in our society.

6: *An Ungovernable Nation*

AMERICANS VIEW nearly all agencies of government as inherently illegitimate. This distrust, a product of habit and history, not only limits official activity but also allows more latitude for private undertakings than is permitted by any other industrialized nation.

Americans are convinced that hardly an hour passes without some public intrusion into personal lives and fortunes. However, protests against the most innocuous of official incursions can be quite as vociferous as cries accompanying really serious losses of liberty. Indeed, our complaining over every attempt at regulation indicates a basic unwillingness to accept any government initiative at all.

America was founded on the premise that legitimacy

inheres only in private activity. Thus the presumption that every individual may put his money and his property, his energy and ambitions, to uses of his own devising. Those owning land, for example, feel entitled to whatever pleasure or gain they may derive from its utilization. If this leads to the mutilation of a boulevard or the massacre of a skyline, the burden of proof remains on those with the temerity to suggest that private activity should suffer public regulation. (For this reason, of course, the United States has no beautiful cities.) Americans have allowed their governors only the most tenuous powers to plan or control. Fear of "the state" underpins the sentiment that individual freedom must always outrank public policy.

The premise follows that those engaged in production are entitled to decide how goods and services shall be created—even if the by-products are pollution, congestion, and disruption of the nation's demography. Hence, too, the view that those practicing callings such as medicine and law, education and plumbing, may organize the means by which the society will be provided with its health and justice, its learning, and even its bathtubs. Therefore, as well, the conviction that citizens must be permitted to spend their earnings and leisure as and when they choose, select occupations and be allowed to marry and raise families at their own discretion.* In the

* Let me make quite clear that I am by no means referring only to citizens of conservative persuasion. Fewer and fewer Americans seem preoccupied with such symbols as "private property" or "free enterprise." Only a diminishing minority still intone their politics in these accents any longer: most voters show an impressive sophistication in rationalizing their political outlooks. My point, rather, is that the great majority of Americans—liberals and moderates no less than conserva-

127

name of "freedom," Americans have endowed themselves with the inalienable right to clutter the national
landscape with as many automobiles, children, and tin
cans as they see fit.

If Americans are freer of government control than
similar citizenries, their daily groans would lead one to
believe, instead, that they experience an oppression of
intolerable proportions. Any American will without hesi-
tation give a long, unprompted recital of how his government lords over him. If the well-to-do harangue on confiscatory taxes and intrusive regulation of their business
and personal affairs, the poor complain of the pettiness
and impersonality of the bureaucratic agencies. While
local leadership waxes indignant over the incursions of
national authority into their domains, other observers
point with alarm to the nation's military and foreign
commitments. At no time—even in war—are a majority
of Americans at ease over what they perceive to be the
overwhelming scope of their government. But this is
hardly surprising. For government in the United States
was never intended to evoke the confidence of citizens. It
was, on the contrary, created as a necessary but unwanted
presence. Even today it is as though alien agents of

---

tives—share a basic anti-government sentiment. Intellectuals who profess their support for progressive programs are as committed to their
private enjoyments as the most selfish of businessmen. While their
expenditures undoubtly differ—wine as opposed to whisky, stereo-
phonic sound rather than cabin cruisers—they are equally attached
to personal consumption. Moreover, the view that government has
become too large and too intrusive is expressed as much on the left
as on the right wing of politics. In short, I am describing what
amounts to an American consensus: an attitude which transcends ideological variations and which limits the ambit of government, no
matter which party is in office.

George III were still ensconced in public office.

Until quite recently the anarchy of Americans had a certain charm. If government has been weak, and its authority susceptible to obstruction, that did not much matter. The country was sufficiently large, the economy expanding, and individuals found opportunities to make their way through life without guidance by public policy.

Given this happy circumstance of history, America never felt the need for a governing class whose members would devote lives and energies to public careers. Hence, the average American politician has been a local product of unpretentious origins, having the traits and talents to win votes, come to terms with dominant figures in his constituency, and make the rounds of conferences and consultations that would assure him of retaining office. Moreover, the majority of elected officials oppose the idea of purposeful government as their electorate does. Their first commitment is to curbing expenditure, to consolidating prevailing arrangements, to holding the line instead of advancing it. If few politicians gain genuine respect, this is less their failing than the failing of a citizenry unwilling to estimate highly any individual who aspires to political power.

American civil servants have been anonymous functionaries, unable to develop either a commanding presence or a professional stature. In nations less burdened with a democratic mentality, governing classes are accorded the respect and wherewithal they require to carry out public responsibilities. Whether such countries are socialist, liberal, or conservative, their rulers are allowed to govern because citizens acknowledge that the broad exercise of political power belongs to government.

Most other constitutional nations still possess a powerful feudal residue, and as a result those holding public office encounter some measure of popular deference.* This arrangement depends on the willingness of the ordinary citizen to have power exercised over his life and fortunes. Such a tradition is absent in the American democracy.

Thus, government in the United States tends to be an enervated and isolated institution with an extreme and embarrassing vulnerability of all its agencies at whatever level. Executive bureaus and even judicial benches are regarded as outposts to be infiltrated, as offices to be manipulated, or as an enemy camp to be kept in a state of want and prostration.

It is hardly surprising, then, that the political calling wears so low a status. For if government takes the form of an emergency operation having no positive mandate, it will inevitably be staffed by clerks and careerists. Seldom are public officials allowed to take an initiative, for the overriding attitude of society is that government should never innovate. Even the most sophisticated diagnoses of society's ailments—whether atmospheric pollution or juvenile delinquency or the shortage of dentists—begin by averring that improvement ought first to emerge from private circles and the most local of sources. That neither private nor local agencies can or will produce effective

* Of course, electorates in Western Europe criticize the parties in power and, on periodic occasions, vote them out of office. Yet the assumption is that the government of the day has the right to govern and to extend broad authority over activities Americans consider "private."

action on these fronts is already well known. However, the ritual requires expressions of reluctance over public expenditure or expanded bureaucratic intervention. Americans of all ideologies have been firmly schooled in the belief that a government which proceeds with ideas and authority of its own is headed toward totalitarianism.

Perspective is most sorely needed. Those who believe that we live in an age of "big government" would do well to review the lessons they have dutifully learned. Of course America's government has "grown." The most elementary textbooks point out that in revenues and expenditures, in agencies and employees, in augmented activities and expanded responsibilities, government at all levels is larger and more powerful than at any previous time.

Yet the only meaningful way to measure the role of government is by comparing its activities with those of private individuals and institutions. While there have been numberless studies charting the growth of government, no one has ever bothered to calculate the increase in *non*-governmental activity over recent generations. That such estimates have not been attempted is in itself revealing: for such information would undermine the assumption that governmental power looms larger in American life than formerly.

While no guidelines can be devised to measure the rate of increase for all areas of private action, everyday observation indicates that more Americans are now freer to engage in countless activities hitherto outside their experience. Augmented real income has brought greater physical movement: on the roads, in the air, across the water. While new regulations attempt to govern these amenities, the expanded uses individuals find for their boats, cars, and planes outrun all efforts at control. A society with more leisure time and discretionary income necessarily produces more kinetic energy: not only do people jostle one another to a greater degree, but they are also more sensitive to lack of elbow room. In earlier times individuals spent more of their waking hours at work; they were apt to remain in their neighborhoods for most of their lives, and thus created few of the disruptions that accompany mobility. In addition, the multiplication of material goods in private hands causes greater social dislocations, ranging from concern over the quality of meat to the collection and disposal of garbage. As each day passes, public agencies are less able to cope with the problems created by a new abundance of pastimes and acquisitions.

Black Americans were less obtrusive in the past and stayed in what they were told was their proper place. However, they now have a new image of their rights and, in consequence, exhibit a greater boldness as they move through the larger society. This flexing of muscles by a hitherto suppressed class has developed farther and faster than governmental efforts to deal with the implications of racial liberation. And more people are exercising their freedom to marry mates of their own choosing, to dissolve those marriages, and even to have offspring out of wedlock. The enlarged spheres of private activity all combine to affect the nation's mental health, its physical safety, and the quality of its life. The new areas of personal freedom are impressive, but this activity can create dislocations at a rate far exceeding the ability of even an expanded government to cope with them. Each time official power and authority are enlarged, private activity leaps several paces ahead and produces still more aggravated discomforts for society.* The only possible conclusion is that, for all its much publicized "growth," government falls further and further behind in its capacity to discharge the duties for which it continues to be held responsible.

Despite this imbalance, Americans prefer to regard their newly found freedoms as a matter of right. Rather than express appreciation for the opportunities and enjoyments now within reach of the average citizen, they complain about how heavy-handed tax-collectors have brought them to the verge of poverty. Attitudes toward taxes, perhaps more than anything else, reveal the self-centered character of American citizenship.

By tradition, Americans have always been hostile to taxes. One reason why we declared our independence was that Great Britain's monarch had the temerity to send "swarms of officers to harass our people and eat our substance." To be sure, the War of Independence was fought over the principle that taxation without representation was tyranny; however, even after those alien overlords were sent packing, we persisted in the conviction

---

* And, of course, the nation's 500 largest corporations, 50 largest unions, and 20 largest foundations are far more powerful than were their counterparts of a previous generation. Moreover, there is reason to conclude that the amount of power inhering in these private institutions has been growing at a faster rate than has the ability of government to regulate, influence, or control their activities.

that taxation is an act of oppression. ("The power to tax is the power to destroy" has always been one of the most popular tenets of American jurisprudence.) What this rhetoric really expresses is the belief that personal expenditure is the only proper use for the money a man earns. We are not only persuaded that the government which taxes least governs best: we also look upon any rate exceeding a base-point of zero as unjustifiable.

Officeholders are defeated, school budgets rejected, and governmental programs gutted under the never furled banner of "No New Taxes." We have arrived at the point where we consider our liberties in dire jeopardy if tax notices compel us to forgo recarpeting our living rooms or put off a vacation trip to London or Las Vegas.

Nor is it a paradox that complaints over taxes accompany rising prosperity. The more money people make, the more they feel entitled to spend on personal comforts and pleasures. Entry into a higher bracket is regarded as an opportunity not only for a new car and home, but also for a whole new style of life. The prospect of higher tax rates leeches much of the joy out of affluence.

The United States has the world's highest living standard, a condition most visible in our role as private consumers. At the end of the 1960s, we spent $2 billion per year on jewelry (as much as the total Federal budget for the War on Poverty); over $2.5 billion on foreign travel (matching what the fifty states spend on welfare); and no less than $3 billion on pleasure boating (almost double the government's outlay for foreign aid). More than 60,000 families built swimming pools in a single year;

there were more than 1.7 million second homes in the United States; and in less than a decade we laid out over 10,000 new golf courses at a cost exceeding $2 billion (double our annual capital outlay for community water-supply systems). These figures show that citizens have no shortage of after-tax cash.

Every American, poor or prosperous, has a lengthy shopping list at the back of his mind; and any extra cash he earns—or hopes to earn—is earmarked for items on that inventory. Not all of these aspirations are materialist in the literal sense, for the tendency in sophisticated circles has been toward the consumption of services—travel, dining, entertainment—rather than tangible goods. Imagine a citizen who finds himself with an unexpected sum of several thousand dollars: perhaps an inheritance from a relative, a bonus from his employer, or a lucky run at the racetrack. There is little point in arguing with him about how that money might best be spent. For he will have made up his mind about the things he would like to do or buy: a vacation in Hawaii, or a cottage on a lake, air-conditioning in his home, or even an increased portfolio of investments. The basic point remains: we never seem to have enough money for the enjoyments that entice us.

Meanwhile the surrounding society is decaying at an accelerating rate. The list of discomforts is too familiar to warrant elaboration: overcrowded schools and under-staffed hospitals, clogged highways leading to jammed recreation areas, growing slums producing a rising crime rate. When Americans set foot from their homes, they enter an environment that is physically dangerous, aesthetically repellent, and morally disquieting.* The public domain has ceased to be civilized territory.

Nevertheless, there persists an unwillingness to weigh personal comforts and pleasures against anxieties due to inadequate and underfinanced government. Every dollar expended for individual purposes is one withheld from the public purse. All Americans are familiar with this fact of life, which lends emphasis to their insistence that they cannot afford to pay in a penny more in taxes. Indeed, we have devised the most elaborate explanations to prove that the limit has long been reached.

Thus the argument that the nation must wait until it ends its overseas commitments before government can embark on really ambitious domestic programs. Obviously, we have already demonstrated our ability to finance all manner of foreign involvements and, at the same time, live very handsomely at home. The old two-way choice between "guns and butter" is not terribly helpful here: for the sacrifice of "butter" means not the giving up of personal luxuries, but rather the postponement of civic programs. What wars make us relinquish

---

* As citizens begin to experience prosperity, their attitudes and expectations change in such ways as to require *proportionately more* public services. As personal income rises, the ways individuals spend their additional earnings tend to create social problems that did not hitherto exist. In other words, the disruption caused by the expenditure of every new private dollar is more severe than that brought about by the last. Thus when the Gross National Product rises to $1,500 billion—as it surely will—the fraction of that sum going into governmental coffers should be greater than when the GNP was only $800 billion. If, as seems more likely, we insist on keeping our tax rates constant at a fixed proportion of the GNP, then we will find ourselves waiting longer in congested airports, living more restively amid growing mounds of garbage, and sending our children to understaffed and overcrowded colleges.

are not private swimming pools or golf courses or new cars, but rather rebuilt mental hospitals, new prisons, and a decent diet for undernourished schoolchildren.

Much the same can be said of the view that states and localities have reached the limit of their taxing capabilities. Some economists argue that a portion of Federally raised revenues should be returned to the states in the form of block grants; states and communities, this proposal assumes, are closer to the people, and hence will spend those funds more effectively. Yet a consequence of being so "close" to the citizenry is that these governments lack the courage to raise local taxes. The point is not that there is no money left in local taxpayers' pocketbooks—not a few people spend more on wine each year than they do on school taxes—but rather that taxpayers, pleased with the notion that the local wells have run dry, are unwilling to run down a plumb-line.

But the time of reckoning has come. American life has reached the juncture where social dislocations are so great that only the most ambitious of governmental efforts could produce even token exercises in amelioration. The nation's ailments are not particularly new or unique. Poverty and racial discrimination have existed for generations, as have crowding and illness and dirt. Rioting, looting, and urban violence have occurred, albeit episodically, for over a century. But now people demand that these conditions be remedied. Social dissatisfaction always rises when accelerating expectations illuminate the gap between aspiration and reality. Throughout history the majority of the world's inhabitants have lived and died in woeful surroundings, never protesting

137

because they failed to conceive that their condition could be better.

The perceptions of all classes are now sharper, discontents run deeper, with a widening sensation of social injustice. There is not a housewife or a high-school student who cannot rattle off a full schedule of America's domestic difficulties, ranging from an ascending illegitimacy rate to rioting in the streets. Yet all this awareness is accompanied by a continued refusal to mandate effective governmental measures. While part of the reason lies in an abstract fear of an oppressive officialdom, at base stands the unwillingness of citizens to pay the costs.

The United States has only recently become a nation of homeowners and taxpayers. A majority of citizens now have the unsettling experience of seeing a visible fraction of their earnings taken from them in taxes. While these sums are by no means confiscatory, the typical taxpayer has nevertheless concluded that they have reached bankrupting levels. As a result, today's householder of moderate means is even more reluctant to give up a portion of his cash than were the wealthy classes of past generations.*

The fact that a majority of Americans now hold title to their homes is the primary cause of our fiscal crisis. Of

* Complaining about taxes is also a useful social symbol. Graduation to the status of oppressed taxpayer is a sign of success. To be able to wax eloquent over the depredations visited on one's earnings is an acceptable method of proclaiming that you are both a person of property and a pillar of society. While a citizen cannot, without appearing unseemly, inform others of his income ("Last year I made more than $17,000"), he can get that message across by detailing the exactions perpetrated on him by the local assessors ("This year my school tax will be almost $600").

138

all the taxes citizens must pay, most rankling of all are the assessments levied for local purposes. When wage-earning Americans lived in rented quarters, property taxes fell chiefly on the well-to-do. But now that the United States has become a nation of homeowners, the number of discontented taxpayers has risen to majority proportions. Owning one's home has been a focal point of the American dream, and the realization of this goal has swelled the ranks of those opposed to raising the public revenues.

Even now the American people hold to the belief that creativity arises only out of private endeavor. Government is seen solely as a coercive instrument, never adding to the nation's wealth or well-being but rather constricting efforts at innovation originating elsewhere. The average citizen would be hard put to cite even one or two creative acts on the part of public agencies, not because they are difficult to think of but because of an ingrained reluctance to admit that official creativity can exist at all. The government's function is regarded as essentially custodial, tidying up much of the debris created by private pursuits. And while voters and taxpayers may consent to occasional governmental activity in areas private enterprise finds unprofitable, these endeavors are viewed with suspicion and are tolerated only at the economy's margin.

Accordingly, government activities and employees are not expected to exhibit the qualities characteristic of those who labor for a profit. The very expenditure of official money is expected to be less efficient, less economical, and seldom inspired in conception or result. The

legitimacy ascribed to private business is such that few
Americans become aroused over the social consequences
of its manner of operation. If the chimneys of a manufacturing company pollute the air, or the refuse of a paper
mill fouls the waterways, it is virtually impossible to persuade the public that such firms should be held responsible for damage to the environment. The business of producing paper or chemicals is looked upon as necessary,
proper, and self-justifying. Industrial waste is accepted as
a fact of life: there is little inclination to believe that matters could be otherwise. By the same token, no popular
outcries arise over the architecture of office buildings, or
the private construction that misshapes urban areas and
outlying suburbs.* Compare the virtual lack of public response to these private operations with the reaction to
even the most trivial governmental activity. Much more
is written—usually critical—about public housing projects than about the location, appearance, and purpose of
private building.

American ideology possesses neither the language nor

* It is worth noting that the public is willing to pay—unquestion-
ingly and uncomplainingly—all manner of "taxes" imposed by the
nation's giant firms. Concealed in the price of every automobile, dish-
washer, and kilowatt of electricity are profits the company does not
distribute to its stockholders but rather retains for investment purposes. Instead of attempting to raise capital through the money market—an operation that would require them to obtain the "consent" of
would-be investors—large corporations set aside a major portion of
their earnings to underwrite investment. This amount is truly a "tax."
But consumers refuse to regard these levies in this light. Americans
look upon business enterprises—and the "taxes" they exact—as essentially legitimate institutions. The typical middle-class citizen probably
pays almost as much in such "taxes" to corporate America as he does
to government. In the case of the latter he complains as vociferously
as he knows how; with the former, however, he assumes that private
bodies will put his money to legitimate uses.

the inclination for a critical review of the society's private institutions. Ask the average, well-educated citizen to offer some sustained comments on the role and functioning of corporations such as General Motors and General Electric in his society. Apart from a few commonplaces on automobile safety or defective refrigerator handles, he will have nothing to say. If he is asked to evaluate the performance of the president and executives of United States Steel or Union Carbide, he will have no comment, nor will he think it necessary to hold opinions in this area, even though these men possess as much power as the governor of his state or the mayor of his city.

In consequence, virtually all our criticisms are directed toward government. Government is held responsible even for those ills of society which rise out of private activities. And because these criticisms are concentrated on one target, they hit with an exaggerated impact. Hence the unceasing scrutiny, the relentless publicity, the perennial investigation, to which the officials and policies of government are subjected. It is the misfortune of public agencies that they cannot deflect such criticism to other quarries. Labor unions and minority groups also find themselves on the firing-line, but government bureaus receive the brunt of citizen displeasure.

Thus while government is held responsible for social order, it is not permitted to tax accordingly, nor are its officials granted the power to impose some quotient of rationality on a self-centered population. The question therefore arises whether Americans actually want their government to better conditions. Considering the degree to which the public holds it accountable for the short-comings of society, one might conclude that the American people do desire official initiatives. But an ultimate unwillingness to foot the costs—by paying the bills and giving up personal freedoms and pleasures—can only be construed as supporting social drift and public inaction.

America has become an ungovernable nation whose inhabitants refuse to regard themselves as citizens of a social order in which the authority of government plays a principal role. While no society can be totally anarchic, the United States has as powerless a government as any developed nation of the modern world. Americans prefer to see their society as a conglomeration of private individuals and activities entitled to pursue profit and pleasure as they choose. Health, housing, transportation, even relations between races, classes, and sexes are deemed to be private matters: to behave as one pleases in these and countless other areas is a cherished liberty no free citizen will easily relinquish. But most prized of all an American's possessions is his money, and its expropriation for civic purposes must be resisted by all available means.

While the authority of government remains relatively circumscribed, the discourse of public life shows unusual sophistication. Officials and observers now utilize terms that in earlier decades were known only to sociologists. More Americans display an understanding of the dislocations besetting their social lives. They know why riots occur in segregated slums, if not on college campuses; they can say sensible things about poverty, unemployment, and inflation; and issues such as war, sex, and the quality of moral life now tend to be objects of analysis

142

rather than articles of assertion. However, the belief that enhanced understanding will necessarily stir a nation to action is one of mankind's oldest illusions.

Much talk is heard, for example, of the need for purposive leadership. The argument runs that while the American people may be overly self-centered, this condition could be overcome by the emergence of leaders capable of inspiring the citizenry to personal sacrifices for public ends. Yet the fact remains that there arrives a time in a nation's history when its people have lost the capacity for being led. Contemporary Americans simply do not want—and will not accept—political leadership that makes more than marginal demands on their emotions or energies. Thus, for all the eloquence about the need for leadership, Americans are temperamentally unsuited for even a partial merger of personality in pursuit of a common cause. The inflation of 200 million egos thus carries political consequences. A society so inordinately attached to personal pursuits cannot be expected to renounce them simply because social survival demands such an adjustment.

Concern has also been professed over the disappearance of community. America's enormous population, its tempo of human movement, and the rise of impersonal institutions are resulting in yearnings for social arrangements more respectful of individual identity. Hence new calls for decentralization of decision-making, for neighborhood control of public services, for expanded participation in exercises of power. Underlying this talk is the assumption that the American people can be distributed into systems of local communities where they may direct

143

a meaningful portion of their civic destinies.

Interestingly, but not surprisingly, the discussion has been confined to decentralization of public services such as school systems, welfare administration, and police protection. This emphasis again reveals the presumption that the growth of government, particularly at the Federal level, has been the major factor in causing contemporary unease.

However, if most Americans feel powerless, it would be wrong to attribute their frustration to the expanded activities of public bureaus. Even if communities were developed in which their members could help decide how the garbage was collected or what route a new highway would take, individuals would continue to feel almost as helpless and vulnerable as they do now. The chief reason is that the most substantial concentrations of power continue to reside in private institutions: particularly corporate organizations that provide employment, create capital investment, and give shape to the nation's material life. These institutions are not on the list for "community control," nor is it likely that they will be subjected to any but the most marginal of local influences. However, the decisions made by these nongovernmental bodies determine how large numbers of Americans will lead their lives; and feelings of powerlessness will persist so long as corporations are allowed to carry out programs at their own discretion. The dispersal of govenmental functions may or may not achieve some small measure of citizen satisfaction.* But such proposals

* It should not be forgotten that some of the most vocal proponents of decentralization are found in state legislatures, city councils, and

attack only the smallest, albeit the most visible, aspect of the problem of power.

A far more critical question is whether the American character has become incapacitated for community membership. For the stability and satisfactions of traditional communities depended on acceptance of authority, adherence to a moral consensus, and a willingness to subsume one's identity to the communal values. Indeed, independence of mind has always been the great enemy of community. Too great a presence of individual ambition can damage this fabric, as can too severe a questioning of custom. All lasting communities—whether small towns or ethnic neighborhoods, whether religious or military or corporate in setting—have survived not only due to their coherent identities but also because their adherents have been willing to delegate authority to those in power. (Even New England villages had a local class which exercised ongoing power and to which less prepossessing citizens deferred when important decisions were made.) In fact, the typical community has been built on a relatively rigid class system, with each member knowing and accepting his place. Americans have always preferred to ignore this aspect, even though it is the main

---

local business communities. These worthies realize that state and local agencies tend to be more sympathetic to middle-class and business interests than is the Federal government. For them "community control" is simply an updating of the venerable "states' rights" battle cry, an arrangement whereby those already in positions of privilege can co-opt official policy in informal and unpublicized ways. Thus there is no guarantee whatever that reducing the Federal government's role will actually give power back to ordinary neighborhood citizens. They may have a *chance* to take the reins: but only by exercising continual political leverage, an activity uncongenial to most Americans of modest circumstances.

reason why millions of bright but lowly born individuals leave such settings for places where talents are appreciated. Community membership may be either a voluntary matter (as, for example, with those who choose a career as officers in the military services) or it may persist simply because a person knows no alternative (as, for example, those born and raised on Mennonite farms or in Hasidic slums).

Yet very few Americans are now willing or able to constrict their personalities to dimensions compatible with such a life. Most people estimate their opinions too highly to adhere to any consensus, let alone one involving common goals. Moreover, authority tends to be regarded with suspicion, and all codes are continually questioned. Americans remain restless and self-centered, giving priority to individual pursuits and advancement. (Thus, even the most sociable of suburbs are not and never will be communities in any but the most superficial sense.)

All this requires emphasis if only because individuals of varying ideologies continue to call for a restoration of community. Antediluvian conservatives would have the nation revert to the values of small-town America, combining patriotism, piety, and parental authority with the virtues of private enterprise and individual initiative. Those more radical would abolish both competition and capitalism, replacing them with a series of settlements where alienation has vanished and material incentives and illegitimate power no longer corrupt the human spirit. But both these dreams need for their fulfillment a personality far different from that now present in the American character. The conservative community demands habits of deference found only in individuals who can remain content in a status not of their own making. The radical community requires an altruism untainted by private property or individual ambition.

However, neither of these ideals has historical relevance or political application. Each, in its own way, understands the social cost of technological innovation. But this is a technological age, and it exacts a price that must be paid. The conservative approach to community is essentially pre-industrial, a pastoral idyll updated with white picket fences. (Needless to say, those attached to this vision see themselves occupying the manor house rather than the plowman's cottage.) The radical community lies in a post-industrial future: machines are not to be abolished but rather relegated to distant locations so society can have the comforts of technology and at the same time remain uncontaminated by exposure to industrial organization.

The current search for community has come at the wrong time, addressed to the wrong audience. This conversation seeks to confront the obvious gulf between reality and a world we would like to know. Yet the United States lacks the basic requisites—human, social, historical—for developing community life either in this generation or in the several to follow. Indeed, those who talk most eloquently on this topic, whether from the left or the right, are the least qualified of all for spending their lives in such settings.

7: Ideology and Self-Indulgence

AMERICA'S LIBERALS hardly rank among the nation's dispossessed. On the contrary, they enjoy middle-class incomes and education, and tend toward the conversational professions rather than business or technical occupations. Yet, far from defending their social class or the system whose rewards they have reaped, they call for programs that would endanger the very eminences they occupy.

Why do individuals of superior rank and substantial earnings press for changes that would jeopardize their unique positions? To advocate extended rights and economic equality implies a willingness to share possessions and privileges with the less fortunate. These qualities of conscience and compassion obviously deserve some dis-

cussion, even though it is difficult—perhaps impossible—
to ascertain exactly how such sentiments develop.*

Most middle-class liberals feel some degree of guilt
over privileges they attribute to accidents of birth. They
realize they have done little to entitle them to their good
fortune, and, unlike their conservative cousins, they are
reluctant to rationalize the status they enjoy. As has been
emphasized, only a minority of middle-class Americans
suffer this unease of conscience. But in every period of
history some of the offspring of middle- or upper-class
parentage refuse to defend the system in whose bosom
they were reared. Children of privilege, they seek to ex-
piate their sins by siding with the oppressed classes.

Indeed, an implicit assumption of liberalism has been
that every society possesses a class whose hour in history
is about to arrive. At any given time one may identify a
group ready to claim the power and position it has hitherto been denied. Accordingly, the liberal's mission is to
locate those victims of oppression scheduled for a ren-
dezvous with history. Put most simply, he seeks to stake
out reservations for himself in a movement due for a shift
in status.

Thus, despite the changing content of liberalism, its
continuity as an ideology lies in identification with classes
about to enter their ascendancy. In the nineteenth century, liberals enlisted on the side of the rough-hewn en-

---

* It is common knowledge that Jews are more apt to be liberals than
are Christians, that more Episcopalians will hold liberal views than
will Baptists, that professors of sociology are more likely to be found
on the left than chemical engineers. However, enough Jews, Episcopalians, and professors are *not* liberals to make one wonder what in
a person's experience leads him in one or another ideological direction.

trepreneur in his struggles against aristocratic privilege. The major spokesmen for laissez-faire and limited government were academics and intellectuals who had little in common with mill-owners and tradesmen, but who sensed that the future belonged to the businessman. To be ideologically allied with the side that would ultimately win was sufficient justification for moral commitment.

For the same reason, subsequent generations of liberals identified with the exploited proletariat. They advocated the use of governmental agencies to improve the condition of strikers, sharecroppers, and the unemployed. Here, liberalism's motivation lay in the conviction that the time was ripe for the arrival of the working class.

When classical liberals wished to restrict the functions of government, they took this position because official power frustrated entrepreneurial ambitions. And when later liberals exhibited few trepidations over expanding governmental activity, they reasoned that government could serve as a vehicle for economic redistribution and social reform. What the two liberalisms shared was not a single theory of public policy but rather an identification with classes scheduled to move into the sun.

Now that most members of the working class are no longer poor or powerless, the liberal must find a new historical vanguard. Hence the burst of compassion for black Americans. While there is concern over endemic poverty, it is noteworthy that impoverished white Americans fail to rouse liberal emotions to nearly the same degree as the plight of poor blacks. Liberal sentiments have always been selective, choosing their objects of compassion with a careful eye for the tenor of the times.

Racial minorities will occupy this special position only so long as they qualify as society's downtrodden classes.

Liberal ideology also exalts the presumed potentialities of the oppressed. Untutored businessmen of a bygone era, industrial workers of subsequent decades, and black citizens at the current time have in turn been pictured as uncorrupted creatures whose inherent qualities would become manifest once they were liberated from the shackles holding them down. Folk wisdom, strength of character, and, indeed, a benign nature thus reside within the man enchained. To victims of injustice are attributed capacities more elevated than those of the classes they are slated to replace.

Only by believing in the superiority of the deprived and the powerless can liberalism follow its mission with conviction. Moreover, the liberal may suspect that he has been tainted by unearned comforts and class-imposed repressions; one way of expunging such infections is to identify with those seen as exempt from the corrupting results of affluence.

Yet the liberal always suffers ingratitude once the class he has championed succeeds in bettering its condition. Its members soon lose the virtues liberalism has ascribed to them. The energy and individualism of the rising businessman lost their luster when he used his position to exploit others less energetic or individualistic. Even more instructive was liberalism's betrayal at the hands of the proletariat. The abolition of subsistence wages and insecure employment was expected to usher in a new age of tolerance, culture, and civility. However, the working classes were never informed of this, and, having risen to comfort and security, they developed attitudes as self-centered and short-sighted as those of their erstwhile exploiters.*

The liberal image of man's inherent altruism is repeatedly contradicted when those who were once society's downtrodden refuse to display compassion for citizens afflicted by the same injustices they themselves have managed to escape. Instead of embracing the ideology that once assisted them—which would call for sharing their success with others less fortunate—they strive to keep taxes down, the blacks out, and their own newly won status secure. (While most self-made men tend toward selfishness, a society can survive their quotient of callousness so long as only a few individuals earn fortunes in their own lifetimes. But the consequences can be rather more damaging if whole classes ascend to new heights.)

Yet, for all this, liberals remain undaunted. Each newly chosen class is seen as having qualities that will save it from the corruptions that befell its predecessors. Nevertheless, it will be most surprising if black Americans who achieve some measure of material success do not take their turn at betraying the liberal dream. Within a generation more and more black citizens will

---

* Recall, for example, the nobility invested in the Joads—not only by Steinbeck but also by the millions of middle-class liberals who read *The Grapes of Wrath*. The Joads' innate decency survived even the most harrowing of experiences, giving promise of real fulfillment if only they could find steady employment. Yet where is Tom Joad today? He lives in suburban Los Angeles, has a good job in the aerospace industry, and devotes his energies to protesting welfare programs and keeping non-whites out of his neighborhood.

sit on their suburban patios bemoaning welfare costs and the uncivil conduct of those left behind in the slums. However, the liberal does not want to be warned. He needs his vision of a kindly black nature far more than blacks need such an uninvited attribution.

If most Americans see themselves as possessing superior qualities—an assessment most evident when they are dilating on the shortcomings of classes considered inferior—a liberal may not admit to such self-esteem. For liberalism is an equalitarian ideology: thus, when addressing society's unsuccessful, the liberal must always assert, "You are just as good as I am." Nevertheless, his manner reveals the conviction that those who receive his ministrations are in fact incapable of determining their own destinies. Only those with the language and logic which come from formal schooling can lead others toward social amelioration. (This is certainly a key assumption among social workers and city planners, and the outlook persists with most of those having occupational contact with the poor—not excluding teachers.) More than that, the liberal grows indignant when his role as spokesman is questioned. After all, has he not given of his name and money, his effort and fervor? Do not these gifts entitle him to gratitude?

Until quite recently liberals have been allowed to act out their ideology through financial donations and occasional committee memberships, with perhaps some practical involvement when their schedules permitted. In the past such service was sufficient, for those who were aided imposed no tests on their patrons' sincerity. Liberal assistance was received with gratitude by classes not yet ready to question the methods or motives of those offering help.

But now poor Americans have discovered the limits of liberal involvement. For example, consider the matter of money. Checkbooks snap shut as soon as a cause liberals have supported begins to develop a leadership disinclined to express appreciation for absentee advice. Liberals who have helped to underwrite the rent for this committee or the telephone bill for that association like to feel they have purchased a voice in the group's policies. While support may be withdrawn more in sorrow than in anger, the reasons for liberal disaffections are not lost on those who have the temerity to act on their own principles.

Also integral to liberal reasoning are the endless calls for public expenditures: to rebuild slums and build new schools; to rehabilitate broken families and motivate miseducated children; to provide full employment and expunge the causes of crime and disorder. But programs of this magnitude would require substantial tax increases for middle-class Americans, and liberals—like all others in middle-class America—enjoy the gratifications of prosperity. The liberal is no more attracted to asceticism than is the conservative; the only difference lies in their objects of expenditure. Thus, the liberal needs his stereo set and record collection, his wines and food and foreign travel, his summer home and up-to-date wardrobe. Nor is he inclined to foreshorten this style of life by paying more taxes. The liberal rhetoric implies that sacrifices must be imposed on those who live well, but his attachment to the material life makes clear—certainly to those who are forced to live without such comforts—that he has a great deal in common with his conservative cousins when it comes to giving up personal amenities.*

An even more critical impasse concerns the liberal attachment to procedures, and especially those intended to protect middle-class privileges: due process, formal applications, professional standards, and prescribed channels for appeal. The specters of mob rule, unqualified personnel, and the entire vocabulary of violence send tremors down most liberals' spines. For not only are their own positions and rights challenged by these threats but —and here lies the heart of the matter—the ideology of liberalism emerges as completely unequipped to deal with such stirrings. The whole liberal edifice has always depended on a substratum of social controls, although its ideology preferred to act as if these mechanisms did not exist. Whereas conservatives explicitly admit the need for repression, the liberal simply assumes that most citizens—including the under-aged and the underprivileged —will agree to established procedures. Hence the liberal's frustration when faced with disorders on college campuses or crime in urban streets. And now that forbearance and persuasion are less common, the majority of

* One amenity the liberal is unwilling to share is his physical safety. Liberals—like all members of the middle class—live and work in locations where the chances of assault are substantially lower than elsewhere in metropolitan areas. (To be sure, such individuals will insist that their neighborhoods are terribly unsafe, but they are bastions of security when compared with where the poor live.) However, any redeployment of currently available police protection to benefit higher-crime areas would increase the liberal's own vulnerability. Thus, while he may join in calling for more and better-paid police, he displays no inclination to give up any part of the safety he currently enjoys.

liberals find themselves advocating measures hitherto suggested only in conservative circles. Liberals would, of course, like nothing better than to champion the cause of the young or to assist people charged with crime. However, those who overstep the bounds of liberal approbation find that they forfeit any claims to sympathy and assistance. That this boundary line runs parallel to middle-class interests reveals fully as much about the compass of contemporary liberalism as it does about the behavior of those unimpressed with its dictates.

In sum, the liberal's involvement must be on terms of his own choosing. Even those having some daylight contact with the poor flee to the safety of their own neighborhoods once working hours are over. Similarly, young people who put in a few months or a year on some project intended to alleviate the condition of the underprivileged depart for middle-class universities or careers when that assignment has ended. While they may spend a period in a slum or a migrant camp or on an Indian reservation, their life lies elsewhere; and the very fact that they have this avenue of escape creates resentments that in the past went unvoiced.

The implicit pre-condition of the liberal's commitment, then, is that he be permitted to act out his ideological role with no great inconvenience to himself. The typical liberal is neither a hero nor a martyr, and will not enlist more than a small segment of his life (and that largely verbal) in causes he professes to support. If the dispossessed of earlier generations were less ready to judge those who wished them well, the social controls that instilled this appreciation have all but eroded. But despite such episodes of disillusionment, liberals will continue their quest for classes and causes with which to identify. Essentially an exercise in middle-class self-indulgence, liberalism is a mode of expression for comfortably situated citizens who wish to appear progressive in outlook without having to pay too high a price for their principles.

8: The Illusion of
Individuality

AMONG THE MORE widespread postwar preoccupations
has been the growing impersonality of life in America.
While the major causes will turn on each commentator's
disposition, most agree that rootlessness, alienation, and a
crisis of identity characterize the time. Confused over
goals and values, and no longer capable of establishing
meaningful relationships with one another, Americans
find themselves powerless and frustrated appendages in
an age of dehumanized institutions.

My interest in this chapter will be to inquire why criticism of this sort has evoked such a strong response. One
reason is that these commentaries depict much that is true
about postwar America. Mass production, mass consumption, and the mass media; specialization, seculariza-

tion, and suburbanization; the growth of government, of corporate capitalism, and of messianic militarism—these are all clear and present conditions having deep-seated effects on the attitudes of Americans. However, the social structure and economic development of any society leave a mark on the character of its citizens. What is different here is the intensity of concern over the status and predicament of "the individual."

While philosophers have been locating "the individual" at the center of their systems for several centuries, it is only recently that this emphasis has entered the vernacular. When a society's population consists mainly of peasants or proletarians, only a small minority can voice the theory of individuality. However, most Americans, now liberated from the confines of rural bondage and industrial exploitation, have embraced an outlook that was once the property of an elite few. Thus, today virtually everyone looks upon himself as an "individual." For with new occupations, enhanced education, and liberation from constricting surroundings, people formulate new conceptions of themselves and their hitherto hidden potentialities. Not only do more Americans expect more out of life, but they are also more sensitive to forces pronounced harmful to their newly discovered capacities.

Assertions of individuality, while ideologically understandable, form the basic myth of American democracy. More Americans have attained new jobs, more schooling, and a greater exposure to the variety of what life has to offer. Nevertheless, in major attributes they remain essentially the same sort of people as were their peasant and proletarian forebears. This is to suggest not only that their new conceptions of self have no factual basis—for it would be difficult to show that the materials of which Americans are made have undergone a marked improvement—but also that the average person cannot be expected to live up to the standards he now sets for himself. Moreover, most of the sensations of injustice about which citizens complain arise from overinflated hopes concerning what an ordinary person may experience throughout his life.

But because assumptions are not examined, even the most sophisticated commentaries take the view that in more salutary circumstances American men and women would reveal capacity for outlooks and accomplishments they have not yet achieved. Current attitudes and behavior are seen as corrupted crudescences: for contemporary humanity has been distorted by institutions and imperatives resulting from either accidents of history or the intrigues of those who profit from a maldistribution of power. Were these constrictions to be removed, "the individual"—every man and woman—could ascend to a level of life where their potentialities for a creative existence would reach a full flowering.

But the problem with discussions of human "potentialities" is that no facts support the arguments. The historical record may be used to demonstrate man's inherent good nature, his tendency toward evil, or some mixture of these and other attributes. Equally authoritative evidence can be cited to demonstrate that he has the reason and intelligence to control his destiny, or that he has always drifted in a chartless sea. Indeed, the historical record is irrelevant: for mankind's capabilities have hardly had an opportunity for realization in any society the world has known. Thus, the release of potentialities remains a hope for the future rather than an extrapolation from past performance.

One can only speculate, therefore, about what may reasonably be expected from the people who comprise our present society. Here is an automobile salesman in New Jersey, there a television repairman in Alabama; here is a black teenager in Chicago, there a housewife in suburban San Diego. What capabilities lie dormant in them?

Honest observation indicates that on the whole these Americans—and millions like them—are not extraordinarily intelligent, not terribly ambitious, and tend chiefly to be wrapped up in themselves. But suppose that they were somehow released from the thralldom of salesmanship and racial prejudice, from the destructive life of the slums and the dull domesticity of the suburbs—supposing all this, can it be conceived that such people as these, even given the most encouraging conditions, would display some inherent "individuality"? For it may be that assumptions about unfathomed potentialities are only a myth—an illusion that persists because any serious investigation of its premises may prove hazardous to a nation at a difficult stage in its history.

Most people are ordinary. And ordinary people are ordinary, regardless of the time or society or setting in which they live. Moreover, ordinary people are relatively unintelligent, incapable of abstraction or imagination, lacking any special qualities of talent or creativity. They are for the most part without drive or perseverance; easily discouraged, they prefer the paths of security. Whether slave or serf or sweated worker, most people in the past have displayed these traits. And most who inhabit the present, whether scientist or suburbanite or sophisticate, continue to manifest these tendencies.

This is the human condition. One need not invoke theology, nor is it necessary to assert that man is a creature of evil and tainted with sin. I simply argue that in any society all save an exceptional few will lack the capacity for attainments that transcend the mediocre.

Quite obviously words such as these can carry unpleasant implications. However, allusions to differentials in human talents need not originate in pseudo-genetic doctrines or ideologies intended to flatter members of a particular class, race or nationality. What I mean is that most people—white as well as black, rich no less than poor—are not terribly clever or creative or venturesome. Yet, despite these disclaimers, the mere mention of mediocrity raises problems for democratic rhetoric. Indeed, of all the world's peoples, Americans have the greatest difficulty in facing the fact that human beings can be subjected to qualitative judgments.

Hence the emphasis on "excellence"—a quality Americans are prepared to discover in more people and places than was ever thought possible. While competition often compels the ranking of individuals, this does not discourage the concept that the achievements and products of excellence may be attained by virtually everyone.* To

* To be sure, many middle-class Americans enjoy dilating on the moral and intellectual shortcomings of whole categories of citizens they deem their inferiors. And by the same token not a few Cauca-

inform an American that he has limited intelligence or a sinewless character can only be construed as an insult. Not only does the democratic spirit make it difficult for one person to pass judgment on another; an accompanying presumption is that everyone carries the capacity for excelling in at least several areas of life.

The ideology of individuality—and I purposely use this term—is of comparatively recent origin. Until the last generation or so, the emphasis was on "individualism," and the connotations were almost exclusively economic. Moreover, this doctrine was quite straightforward in its intentions: to exalt the entrepreneur and encourage the quest for profit. Hence the qualities it celebrated: a willingness to put aside current earnings and defer gratifications; a readiness to risk these savings in an enterprise of one's own creation; and the determination to make that enterprise succeed by hard work, native wit, and the seizing of opportunities. For all these requisites, those who succeeded were hardly exemplary figures by contemporary standards. Rough-hewn and self-centered, they displayed a bare minimum of moral awareness and eschewed any notions of social responsibility. Patronizing the arts and supporting civic causes earned esteem in certain circles, but such activities were by no means expected by the individualist ethic. One could achieve that

---

sians find it difficult to discover potentialities in persons more darkly hued than themselves. Yet, despite the standards they set for others, such individuals attribute quite flattering qualities and accomplishments to members of their own race and class. Perhaps, then, it would be more accurate to say that it is *within* their own races and classes that Americans display their magnanimity toward one another's capacities.

status simply by building or enlarging an enterprise that surpassed and outlasted the efforts of others.

Current assumptions require that expressions of individuality be more than economic. However, any attempt to extend an ideology of this sort to non-economic areas encounters serious difficulties. For, while success in entrepreneurial individualism lay solely in how much money a self-made man might amass, no methods have been devised for assessing or identifying qualities unsusceptible to monetary measurement. What one person will see as a genuine philosophical talent, another will perceive as exhibitionism or eccentricity. Where some will detect a statesmanlike courage, others will find opportunism and expediency. (Certainly not all departures from convention can be construed as evidence of praiseworthy qualities. Why else has the term "neurotic" become so common?) Because of the impossibility of agreeing on its attributes, the democratic resolution has been to bestow candidacy for individuality on everyone.

Clashes over definitions fail to impress middle-class Americans, who remain persuaded that with just a little more effort and some added insight they may discover their true selves. Thus the growing commitment to education, and the conviction that with schooling can come not only wordly success but also an awareness of one's own potentialities. Yet the majority content themselves with unexamined assumptions: one is that what happens in classrooms has an influence on subsequent behavior. Yet, on the whole, the educational process has surprisingly little effect in determining how people will finally shape their lives. Apart from technical training, what ed-

164

ucation imparts is chiefly a set of perceptions through which the world may be seen, plus a vocabulary for describing that vista. The process may occasionally instill values or induce feelings of guilt, although this is far rarer than most would like to believe. And while there can be no denying that augmented schooling can awaken both a consciousness of style and a sophistication of manner, these are chiefly lessons in how to make the most of prevailing conditions.

Certainly the overwhelming majority of college graduates—presumably the class from which the most should be expected—show little in their lives which can reasonably be called individuality. Despite their exposure to higher education and their heightened awareness of life's options, they nevertheless take paths of least resistance when faced with critical decisions throughout their lives. What their education gives them is the ability to rationalize these choices: a series of verbal strategies for justifying their actions to others and for making peace with themselves.*

* What about the liberal-arts curriculum, which a growing number of Americans elect to study? Quite clearly, most students still go to college to secure credentials for the status and occupations of middle-class careers. Even so, a rising proportion of undergraduates evidence genuine eagerness for a critical understanding of themselves and their world. During these years of suspended animation they can be a real pleasure to teach: their eyes are opened; they ask interesting and important questions; they begin to abandon the cautionary maxims that hitherto held their minds in check.

However, this is an interlude in their lives. For the years of liberal learning cannot extend into the time when careers must be chosen and bargains struck with the arbiters of promotion. This is one reason why professors show little enthusiasm for meeting those students later on. For minds that were once inquiring have now settled into place; and the verbal skills learned in the liberal arts are deployed to defend compromises and accommodations.

Neither the information in a person's head nor the values in his conscience have much to do with his behavior. The principal determinant of human action stems from the fact that most people lack the courage to take chances. Learning lessons of right conduct has become an academic exercise; but conversations of this sort are incapable of instilling the self-confidence needed to pursue even the most noble principles. Americans who have experienced higher education find themselves especially vulnerable because society offers them an array of ascending opportunities—on the condition that they conform to the codes set by those who bestow the material rewards and symbols of success. In short, the college graduate, more than others, has a great deal to gain by being the sort of person others want him to be. And in this situation all talk of inculcating individuality has little meaning.* The one trait America's educational institutions cannot teach is personal courage, and the one quality they cannot abscind is human weakness. Considering the prizes held out to those educated for future success, it

* It is, of course, easy enough to solve the problem simply by debasing the coinage of individuality. Anyone who wishes to discover uniqueness in every member of a community can achieve this end by inflating small talents and marginal distinctions: this woman has a unique recipe for angel cake, that housewife knits her husband's neckties; this man rides to work on a bicycle, that one collects old circus posters; he plays a fine game of golf, she set a shorthand speed record, and they vacationed on a barge canal. Perhaps something is gained in telling the orthodox that they are unconventional, by persuading the weak that they are creatures of courage. Such fictions may obviate the endemic envy of the average and impart a veneer of romance to lackluster lives. Certainly most of those choosing to congratulate everyman on his individuality understand that they tell gentle lies. Perhaps no great harm results from these exercises, except that they encourage the unexceptional to believe that all avocations are of equal quality.

166

should not be surprising that so many strike the bargains they do.

Even if the United States could end poverty and bigotry, diffuse its pyramids of power, and suppress its imperial tendencies, there is no reason to believe that such a society would contain a greater quotient of talented people. For talent has always been, and will always be, a scarce commodity.

Recall for a moment the classical literature of Utopia: portrayals of a benign future where the authors have caused the pressures of contemporary life to disappear. But then take a closer look at the characters who inhabit these idyllic communities. While they are polite, sensible, and socially responsible, most also emerge as very ordinary and unprepossessing people. Even the creators of Utopia, free to devise any manner of population, avoided creating societies of philosophers, artists, and heroes. Perhaps they realized that even in Utopian circumstances the majority of citizens would remain unexceptional. (They may also have suspected that too many talents would strain the community structure.) And in so doing most Utopians have been eminently realistic: their aim has been to make men happy rather than to elevate their aptitudes.

In the past, ordinary people thought of themselves in unpretentious terms, acknowledging their limitations and accepting stations relatively consonant with their capacities. But the emergence of individuality has changed self-conceptions, creating discontents of a sort that were unlikely to occur to men and women of earlier eras. Once persuaded that he is an "individual" entitled to realize his assumed potentialities, a citizen will diagnose himself as suffering quite impressive afflictions.

The intensity with which Americans now explore their egos arises from the conviction that even an average personality is a deep and unparalleled mechanism. Whether psychoanalytic or existential in emphasis, people take pleasure in examining the quality of their "relationships" and achieving an "insight" into their own internal functioning. The heightened concern over sex derives in no small measure from a search for one's "real self" and attempts to find realization through close contact with another person. Hence also the stress on individual "powerlessness," and the constrictions that large institutions impose on self-discovery and self-development. While these terms of discourse are not of recent invention, their employment by so large a part of society is certainly new. Alienation, powerlessness, and crises of identity come into being only if citizens decide to invest their personalities with potentialities ripe for liberation. As soon as people make such decisions about themselves, regulations once taken for granted appear as oppressive instruments of government and society.

Thus, most of those who describe themselves as "alienated" lack any credentials for so tragic a predicament. Given the unexceptional quality and character of the vast majority of Americans, it should be apparent that, however painful the problems they encounter, little is gained by inflating their troubles to traumatic proportions. The average college student—or factory worker or welfare recipient—may indeed feel pushed around, robbed of dignity, or consigned to a status incommensurate with his talents. But to call him "alienated" assumes that if he were liberated from constraints that now annoy him, he would emerge as a different person. To be sure, millions of Americans live at a subsistence level, while others face arbitrary and irrational discriminations throughout their lives. The grievance of such persons is that they have been deprived of experiences enjoyed by people really no different from themselves. To say that you wish to enjoy amenities now available to others ought to be a sufficient argument for eliminating inequality. Considering the behavior of those who have achieved such privileges, the claim that sharing these enjoyments will enhance one's humanity remains a most precarious proposition.

The notion that modern society thwarts self-discovery, compelling people to don masks and distort their true personalities, carries a series of parallel assumptions. However, the fact that so many Americans have become absorbed with asking "Who am I?" need not be construed as evidence of a nationwide "identity crisis." On the contrary, it shows that citizens now feel entitled to give their personal problems philosophical connotations. Self-indulgence of this sort merely indicates that Americans have expanded their vocabularies: it does not mean that these self-estimates have much to do with reality.

To ask "Who am I?" is really rather presumptious. In actual fact, people may still be summed up largely by the roles they fill in society—housewife or husband, soldier or salesman, student or scientist—and by the qualities others ascribe to them: a person "is" black or blind, fat or feminine, indolent or efficient. No one likes being "identified" as simply a fat salesman or a black housewife, and of course the list of a person's roles and characteristics can be extended, but it remains an inventory of attributes externally imposed. Quite clearly many Americans prefer to believe that beneath all the labels lies a unique and identifiable self. Unfortunately for them, the "Who am I?" question can never be answered except in inventoried terms. But the fact that people persist in asking it shows how a little learning can disrupt sensibilities and produce crises unknown in less literate days.

Nor should society be blamed for these problems, particularly those afflicting members of the middle class who complain about restrictions imposed by their communities and careers. It is quite disingenuous to maintain that society forces anyone to be or become anything at all. A person still has the freedom to decide whether or not he will compromise with the world of rewards. If he wishes the comfort and security available to those who join this game, then he will be required to follow certain rules. Those opting for "success" will of course have to adjust to occupational and organizational imperatives. But no one is compelled to enter this gamut. If an individual elects to live an anonymous and unexposed life, if he chooses to stand apart from competitive pressures, then his personality will be left alone. American society has plenty of such places; of course the jobs they offer tend to be uninteresting and poorly paid. Many people obviously want the best of both worlds: material and social success and the freedom to indulge their idiosyncrasies. But it is difficult to muster sympathy for those who complain about the costs of competition. A society that distributes the good things of life with an uneven hand should require some sacrifice of those who reap its rewards.*

Anxieties over problems such as "alienation" and "identity" will continue to preoccupy Americans, for each year more people develop a heightened sense of their own importance. Feelings of isolation and injustice, of powerlessness and oppression, will become more exacerbated among all classes as people expand the enjoyments they consider their due. A people so impressed with their entitlements cannot be expected to revert to simpler settings, to codes and conventions that would prevent the ills they now say they suffer. Skeptical toward all authority and made restive by an encapsulated existence, Americans have divested themselves of the attitudes required for a more commonplace contentment.

The difficulty is that, for all their verbal facility, the great majority of Americans are basically no different from their forebears who lived with a minimum of self-created dilemmas. As contemporary citizens have no

* If I may digress for a moment, I would like to apply this general observation to a quite different question: Who is to be held responsible for wartime atrocities? Every soldier can plead that he was simply following orders, in which case only a single national leader can ultimately be blamed. However, an alternative answer would divide any military force into those who apply for or accept promotions, and those who don't. Individuals who seek or accept elevation above the rank of conscript in effect give their consent to the regime and its works. In taking the rewards it offers, they become tacit participants and acquiesce in its acts. No one has to accept promotion; no private soldier is penalized for choosing to remain a private. Hence, guilt for war crimes should be ascribed to everyone, from corporal to field marshal, who elects to succeed under the regime. Having opted to do as well as they could in the system, such persons cannot complain if they are held as consenting members and hence answerable for its atrocities.

higher an endowment of quality or character than did their less literate predecessors, it remains only to say that pursuit of an ephemeral individuality will certainly increase their frustrations. It is a symptom of our age that people invest themselves with grand attributes, even though they lack the talent or perseverance to realize potentialities they have convinced themselves they have. Hence the need for the illusion of individuality. For this fragile myth is the only support that remains for uncertain spirits in their quest for self-respect.

9: Domestic Dissonance

AMERICAN MARRIAGES cannot be counted among the nation's more successful institutions. Not only do a high proportion end in divorce or desertion, but few of those which continue intact are love-filled or light-hearted relationships. And the most significant catalysts of discontent clearly derive from the dissatisfactions of American wives, for most husbands still prefer the traditional domestic relationship. Despite his claim to value intelligence and imagination in a partner, the modern husband differs little from his grandfather: wifely intelligence should be applied to appreciating his viewpoint, her imagination to anticipating his needs. American women can no longer accept this attitude with equanimity. The years consumed by marriage now give rise to greater frustration; for while domestic arrangements remain unchanged, wives have come to expect far more from their adult lives than did women in the past.

Marriages of earlier eras were durable alliances because a complex of constraints assigned wives to a subordinate position. Religion and community united to persuade half the population that submission was its rightful role. Outward appearances of contentment could be attributed not to notable kindness or consideration between husband and wife but rather to the fact that all surrounding agencies agreed on what constituted the proper relationship between spouses. Thus, the authority of the husband depended less on his physical strength or moral rectitude than on a social and religious consensus that supported his position of dominance.

For all the injustice in marriages of the past, at least they were governed by rules that both partners acknowledged. But the growing reluctance of more and more American wives to accept the double standard imposed by outside authorities has forced married couples to devise guidelines for themselves. Unfortunately, most adults lack the capacity for so bewildering an enterprise. This does not imply that husbands and wives showed more intelligence or intuition in earlier eras. Marital success now calls for unselfishness and sensitivity that the average person simply does not have.

Moreover, a virtual laissez-faire now surrounds the institution of marriage. Americans may marry anyone they choose, using whatever criteria they happen to find convenient at the time. Parental approval is no longer necessary; indeed, couples feel no need to ask advice of any sort concerning the suitability of their intended mates. Marriages also now occur at an earlier age, which means that spouses are chosen with little or no awareness of exigencies attending adult life. The condition of laissez-faire continues after consummation, and it is assumed that wife and husband can learn to live together in close quarters, mustering the required ingenuity without outside help. The nation has priests and physicians, counselors and columnists ready to give advice on how to solve problems. But most individuals are unwilling to invest these experts with anything more than ephemeral authority.

If the classic defense of free enterprise was that survival of the fittest resulted in greater wealth and well-being for the entire society, it was nonetheless agreed that an individual who failed as a businessman was not irretrievably damaged as a productive person. Yet not much evidence can be gathered to show that laissez-faire in marriage produces either maximum social benefits or minimum injury to its participants. Not only can an ill-conceived marriage lay waste a significant span of a person's life, but when a husband walks out on his wife and children, society will probably have to subsidize the home he leaves behind. Millions of American youngsters now grow up in households where the parental relation has become a dull and joyless routine, often infected by bitterness and frustration. Far more serious consequences attend most children raised in fatherless surroundings: finding themselves subjected to society's disdain, they frequently pay back an uncaring community in destructive ways. However, even those willing to acknowledge the social and human costs of ill-judged marriages seem reluctant to propose intervention. (For example: legislating a minimum age for marriage, perhaps as high as twenty-five.) Most Americans can now discuss public regulation of private enterprise without emotional overtones, but programs designed to avert domestic disasters still meet the challenge that the personal realm must be safeguarded from official intrusions.

American men are somewhat more considerate than in the past, but as husbands they still expect to be the focal point of the partnership, and assume that the alliance's major purpose is to support their productive capacities and sustain their personal esteem. Husbandly primacy is taken for granted, with the corollary that a wife's duties must be complementary in character. For all the talk of equality of the sexes, major domestic decisions reflect the needs of the husband and the life he has charted for himself. But whereas both his status and outlook remain substantially as in the past, his spouse's frame of mind has undergone some unsettling alterations.

If American women were unequivocally equalitarian in their aspirations, then many of the present-day stresses would rise to the surface as a clear-cut confrontation between the sexes. However, most women find themselves caught in a dialectical quandary between their traditional conditioning and modern expectations.

One of man's earliest accomplishments was inventing the arrangement whereby the opinions and energies of half the population could be carefully controlled. The qualities and characteristics society ascribes to women were plausible when most females were pregnant from late adolescence through their mid-adult years; childbirth and its aftermath clearly disqualified them from many activities outside the domestic area. Yet that historical circumstance has been loaded with unexamined emotional, psychological, and even physiological assumptions.

Yet it seems self-evident that women and men have about the same range of abilities in performing the tasks now needed by society: in talent, intelligence, and perseverance, any distinctions emerge as marginal or even irrelevant. Certainly the single circumstance of childbearing has become a trivial touchstone for discrimination. A woman's movements may be limited for a few weeks before and perhaps a month or so after childbirth, and assuming that she bears two or three children in her lifetime, it follows that she is debarred from routine activities for less than ten months out of the six hundred which span her age from eighteen to sixty-five. Were all other things equal—which they most surely are not—a married woman would be as available as any man for worldly participation during 98 percent of her adult years.

Arithmetic of this order still remains an academic exercise. The heart of the matter lies in women's acceptance of the definitions that men originally created. The official status of these conventions, the early age at which they are taught and learned, the easy rationalizations for one's role ("I'm glad I'm a girl") all encourage women to believe that they indeed represent the species of humanity men would have them be. To be able to assert "No, it is not so! I am not the creature you say I am!" requires more than creating a new definition. Verbal adroitness is not enough: any effort at innovation in this area also needs some source of legitimacy, if women are to hold these convictions with any self-confidence. Thus, while an increasing number of women resent living a life less than fully human, and while more and more ask embarrassing questions about the role that the culture assigns them, their basic acquiescence deprives them of grounds to suggest an alternative.

Competing on uneven terms calls for a strength of character possessed by few people of either sex. Moreover, there always persists the small suspicion that the official definitions may actually be valid: that Nature really intended women for an auxiliary assignment. As a result, the majority of women end up taking the path of least resistance: marriage and motherhood. Rather than risking unrecoverable years in an attempt to scale male-held battlements, most get married when an early opportunity arises and settle for the pseudo-career of housekeeping and child-raising.

But they no longer do so uncomplainingly. While men enjoy themselves outside the home, those pleasures have become increasingly pyrrhic. In return for access to a wider world, the man—as husband—now suffers greater discomforts at home. Certainly few can any longer count on docility from their wives. More and more women remind both themselves—and their husbands—that only an accident of birth deprives them of freedoms and enjoyments that automatically accrue to even unexceptional men.

Hence the disjunction: American women are not *doing* anything with their lives that differs substantially from what wives and mothers experienced in earlier generations. Women have now developed a new and higher estimate of their human worth, and continued consignment to secondary citizenship engenders frustrations which were usually unfelt or repressed in the past. Such a change in outlook obviously strains so tenuous a relationship as marriage. Dissatisfied American wives make increased demands on their husbands, even if these attacks on his authority seem to lack coherence. Questions once considered closed now become subjects for unending discussion, and in these dialogues the man can no longer assume that he will have the final word.

Despite their equalitarian statements, American husbands are nevertheless unsettled by complaints that seem of doubtful legitimacy as well as diffused and unfocused frustrations. Hence the bewilderment on the part of husbands ("What in hell *is* bothering her?") followed by disgust ("She doesn't know *what* she wants"). But if wives cannot define their restlessness, this is largely because they are unwilling to make critical decisions concerning the opportunities they think are rightfully theirs.*

---

* Imagine for a moment a woman of thirty-two, reasonably educated, and the mother of three young children. Imagine further her dissatisfaction with the preceding dozen years of domestic toil and her dismay over the prospect of at least a dozen more in a similar routine. But then imagine this wife informing her husband that she is tired of wasting her life, that she has decided to embark on a career that always interested her: she intends to finish college, complete professional school, and become a pediatrician—or a city planner or whatever. But, she goes on, she will need her husband's assistance in paying for her education and providing baby-sitters. Moreover, he can no longer count on having a chilled martini waiting when he returns each evening, nor can he assume that his career will still be the central focus of their marriage.

How many American wives, no matter how dissatisfied with their

There are few indications that American women will behave differently in the future. Indeed, with the expansion of the middle class and increasing exposure to higher education, a greater number of wives will express their discontents. While the temptation to romanticize working-class life should always be avoided, in such marriages there tends to be less verbal acrimony over the wife's rights and privileges. (There is much less conversation of any sort in such marriages.) A far higher proportion of working-class wives and mothers go out to work. Such women feel quite free to take unskilled jobs in factories or as waitresses or sales clerks, and their husbands seldom object, because working-class wives and husbands lead relatively separate lives. However, a college-trained engineer employed by a respectable corporation cannot allow his wife to wait on tables at a local diner, and an up-and-coming lawyer would pale at the thought of having his spouse seen as a supermarket check-out girl. The typical middle-class woman finds herself caught in an all-or-nothing proposition: if she wants a career of her own, her employment must have a status approximating her husband's. For this she needs a series of diplomas and credentials, and only a minority are willing to take the domestically disruptive steps required to obtaining them. Consequently, the middle-class wife finds herself socially disqualified from doing anything other than staying at

---

present condition, could make and act on such a decision? And how many American husbands, no matter how seriously they say they take their wives' aspirations, would be willing to see their lives changed in so drastic a way? Indeed, how many American marriages can stand the strain of having two fully fledged human beings living under a single roof?

home, and in this she ends up with less freedom than her working-class sister who spends eight hours a day giving out parking tickets or tending a switchboard.

Americans like to assume that married couples can continue to fulfill their conventional functions. Thus, marriages still bear major responsibility for sex, companionship, child-rearing, and housing and feeding most of the population, even though they lack the strength or stability to carry out these obligations in more than a marginal way. Inertia and vacillation prevent any serious experimentation with agencies that might be preferable in areas where the family has failed.

If marriage leaves much to be desired in the lives of most Americans, the difficulties increase with children. For if men and women no longer understand how to be husbands and wives, they show even more uncertainty as parents. This lack of assurance is intensified by the lack of advice they can regard as authoritative.

Most American parents want to have successful children. Less anxiety would accompany child-raising if mothers and fathers were content to have their sons and daughters remain in a class and condition similar to their own. Adults could then allow their children to observe undemanding standards of behavior. However, not many families welcome the prospect of having immobile offspring. Only the very rich, the very poor, and members of some religious sects and ethnic groups are prepared (or resigned) to having their children grow up as they themselves did. The majority of American parents want their sons and daughters to be successful: in education and in status, through marriage and careers. The success they envisage can be relatively modest, but even an unpretentious advancement from the working class to a white-collar way of life requires passing tests that begin in childhood. Hence the fear that one's children may fail one or another of the hurdles erected by society to make certain that not everyone will succeed.

How does a parent ensure that his children will emerge as successful adults? The advice of one's own parents seems irrelevant, and the precepts of the clergy no longer carry weight. Little comfort is found in conversations with friends and neighbors: while talk of child-raising may be the principal topic when mothers gather, these exchanges reveal only uncertainty and lack of confidence. Hence the search for guidance: the consultations with physicians and teachers, the recourse to handbooks and syndicated specialists. Yet here emerges the ultimate reluctance of Americans to accept professional counsel: not only is it often contradictory, but the suspicion persists that experts in these areas know little more than the layman.

The point is long past when somber head-shaking could arrest the decline of parental authority. If parents in previous generations were able to take a firm stand, it was because society reinforced the sanctions that mothers and fathers chose to impose. In conditions of economic scarcity and religious discipline, it was not all that difficult for parents to keep their sons and daughters in line: the society intervened to help them.

Today, in the slums and in the suburbs, children encounter varying standards from so many different sources that they soon come to regard their parents'

judgment as but one of several valid options. And
through this cacophony of voices they sense that their
own fathers and mothers have become resigned to play-
ing a peripheral role. Early in life children become aware
of their parents' plight. Not only do they perceive the
absence of firm direction, but frequent inquiries about
their own wishes become implicit evidence of their
elders' indecisiveness. (Wander for an hour or so
through any supermarket or shopping center and listen
to mothers with young children in tow. Simple orders
are seldom given. On the contrary, virtually every de-
clarative sentence ends with an upward inflection, the
mother *asking*, ". . . O.K.?" rather than giving an un-
ambiguous command.) *

At the same time, children note their parents' readiness
to acknowledge a putative wisdom in external standards.
By indicating that "everyone" or "all my friends" are
doing this or buying that or going there, parental consent
can as often as not be exacted. Fearful that their sons or
daughters may fall behind in social acceptance, parents
acquiesce if only to ensure that some ingredient of future
success will not be jeopardized. Such easy accommodation soon leads children to perceive that they are investments in which their parents have a high stake. At an
early age they begin to understand the importance of

* It would be a mistake to ascribe current conditions in child-
raising either to popular handbooks or to prevailing philosophies of
education. Theories of "permissiveness" and "progressive education"
are not influences in their own right so much as they are responses to
the new uncertainties of adult America. Giving in to children and
allowing them to express themselves as they choose has gained ground
because mothers and fathers and teachers are no longer sure about
standards of behavior.

their current happiness for their parents' self-esteem. And any investment—most of all a human one—assumes an element of power over those who have an interest in its prosperity.

Americans exhibit more concern over their children's happiness than do parents in any other country. Anger, sullenness, even periods of silence on the part of children create parental discomfiture and are construed as symptoms of failure in child-rearing. (Previous generations of parents did not really care whether or not children were happy. Other attitudes and achievements had higher priority.) Today's adults need a display of smiles each day —even if a price must be paid for these—as reassurance of parental success. Certainly the preoccupation of mothers and fathers with their offspring's happiness has as much to do with their own quest for peace of mind as with the affection they have for the children.

Children now become sophisticated at a far earlier age, urged on by parents who find precocity a useful competitive advantage. Today's youngsters are taken more places and allowed to do and see more things. Accompanying their parents on vacations or watching adult films and television or simply listening in on the conversations of their elders, children emerge with an impressive understanding of the outside world. Most important of all, however, both parents and teachers now encourage evaluation. Factual knowledge no longer suffices; appraisals are both expected and taken seriously. The consequence should not be surprising: a generation so encouraged will sooner or later turn its critical impulses back to their point of origin. Having been urged to consider adult society, children cannot help seeing their own parents as participants in a doubtful morality. Put quite simply, if young people focus on the world's imperfections, they were led to this posture by unwitting adults who praised youthful intelligence and independence.

There have always been clashes between the generations. Children have resented their lack of power and have sought to avoid tasks and obligations they considered unpleasant. But no matter how rebellious they may have been, youngsters in the past seldom *judged* their elders. And this is now occurring. Increasingly beleaguered by their own uncertainties, parents have produced a generation of children who have grown strong by feeding on the insecurities of their elders. Young Americans now possess a self-confidence that transcends their material security. Having been allowed to taste parts of life hitherto the exclusive property of adults, they feel entitled to judge not only the character and quality of their parents' lives but also the entire structure and logic of the world into which they were born.

All this indicates that young people are thinking for themselves. (They are also, of course, thinking of themselves. However, youthful Americans can hardly be said to hold a monopoly on the nation's store of egoism.) Guided less by the goals and prejudices of their parents, and more by their own perceptions and interpretations, they are concluding that adults can no longer claim exclusive custody to truth and reason. While their elders may know the "facts," young people feel qualified to question accepted assumptions. Why should a person transform his personality in order to succeed in a conventional career? Why must individuals forgo assorted experiences—sexual, narcotic, political—until they arrive at an age their elders consider appropriate for experimentation? These questions, moreover, are accompanied by a self-assurance that cannot be dismissed as either arrogance or a passing phase.

Indeed, young Americans have a sharper and more detached understanding of the structure and functioning of their society than do most adults who accept the status quo. As outsiders the young can analyze the motives of those who presume to exercise power. In fact, much of the anxiety that arises over the behavior of young people derives from an uncomfortable awareness that the criticisms are substantially correct. Even those not yet in their teens are far from oblivious to marital infidelity, alcoholic excess, and social opportunism. When they suggest that pre-marital sex, marijuana, and political protest carry less destructive consequences than grown-up pastimes, they speak with a sophistication for which adult America has few confident rebuttals.

Few youthful Americans are so tightly entwined in the world of adult aspirations as to be immune from the ferment in their generation. To be sure, a substantial proportion—especially those raised in working- and lower-middle-class families—still accept the rules of the adult system and dutifully prepare for the careers that society offers to those who have kept their noses and records clean. The country has its quota of conservative young people who refuse to demonstrate against established institutions. A very large number still reject drugs, acquiesce in conscription, and even remain virginal until engaged to be married. Yet the ranks of the sober, the deferential, and the prematurely mature undergo a steady attrition as each year more and more become aware of the enjoyments and immunities available to the young. Young people know full well that they are a "phenomenon." Even those unwilling to engage in open rebellion are prepared to develop a set of values based on their own experience of life.

This, then, is the post-affluent generation. Unlike their parents, who knew scarcity in their youth, most of today's young Americans have known only the material comfort and personal indulgence of postwar affluence. Standards of living have climbed steadily upward as these youngsters have grown from infancy to adolescence, with a rising share of this new abundance lavished on the wants and needs of the younger generation. Their mothers and fathers can recall a time when plenitude was not the rule, and few who have known the experience of the Depression are convinced that there can be such a thing as permanent prosperity. In short, what parents find so difficult to comprehend in their children are the very attitudes produced by having lived only in the postwar period.

Gone are most of the cautionary maxims; and if today's young Americans seem less fearful of consequences, it is because they assume that the security they have always known is built into the foundations of their society. The great difference between the generations—the affluent and the post-affluent—lies in what they take for granted.

Never has the youth of any nation been as secure and self-confident as young Americans at this time. And the liberation they have realized has come about largely because their parents have neither the knowledge nor the will to devise ways of withholding privileges from those still in a state of dependency. One of the strongest controls known to human societies—that of parents over children—has reached its weakest and most tenuous ebb.

Young people have escaped adult influence, and they constitute a community of their own which opens new opportunities for devising styles and circumstances of their choosing.* Here they inform one another on matters of dress and demeanor and about yet-to-be-explored possibilities latent in the emotions and senses. With this generation's temper, there is less need to adopt the internalized repressions that have burdened the lives of their elders. Hence the readiness to engage in pre-marital sex— especially on the part of once inhibited middle-class girls —and the lack of guilt over such liaisons. Hence, too, young men are less preoccupied with the outward appur-

* The term "adolescence" is now heard less frequently, and with good reason. The word used to connote the period from about thirteen to seventeen, when teen-agers made the transition from childhood to adult status. And underlying this term was the assumption that "adolescents" were preparing for adulthood: novitiates learning the rules and repressions of a mature condition. We now speak of "youth," not only as a different age category but also implying a whole new process of development. For "young people" can range all the way from fourteen or fifteen up through twenty-seven and twenty-eight, with not a few of those approaching thirty continuing to claim exemption from the adult regimen. But whether they are fourteen or twenty-eight, and regardless of their dependency on their parents or some other source of adult largess, "young" Americans make their own codes of conduct—which may include participation in activities hitherto reserved for citizens of more advanced years, but on their own terms.

188

tenances of masculinity and more confident of their sexual capacities. This segment of society has the self-confidence to make its own rules; moreover, its members see through the motives of those who oppose youthful independence and innovation, including the ineffectively disguised envy of adults toward the freedoms and privileges their off-spring enjoy.

Young America does not have a coherent ideology of its own. A small minority espouses socialist sentiments, and others call for the rediscovery of community or more genuine participation, but on the whole this generation contents itself with a generalized commitment to world peace, equal justice, and compassion for the downtrodden. Certainly concern is expressed over the hypocrisies that restrain the emotions and stifle the senses. Whether or not such feelings are "radical"—or even political—is less important than understanding that they reflect an awareness of goals and potentialities which existing institutions cannot easily accommodate. Yet young people have little power of the conventional sort, and their hostility to established values will not really influence the conduct of corporate organizations or governmental agencies. At the same time, however, the depth and tenor of these antipathies can create a crisis of legitimacy in otherwise self-satisfied circles. Power will remain much where it has always been; but it will be exercised with less conviction.

Of course, judgments on the economic structure, the political system, and the distribution of wealth and power come easily from a generation thus far insulated from meeting mortgage payments and pursuing corporate careers. Yet the young people's criticisms of self-centered materialism penetrate a vulnerable surface. These assessments of their own parents' lives, coming from a source so close to home, cannot but have a disquieting ring.

Much of the talk heard from young Americans might suggest that they are not nearly so secure as has been indicated. Discussions over campus coffee-cups emphasize fear of alienation, repression, and their powerless condition; by the same token, an impersonal society thwarts meaningful relationships by destroying individuality. If all this talk were true, the youth of this nation would be about as oppressed a class as history has known. However, despite the lamentations, their generation is about the freest in the entire society. Young people do run the risks of police harassment and court-imposed penalties. Subjection to armed service can enervate several otherwise enjoyable years, and restrictions imposed by school principals and college administrators can be onerous and irrational. Yet when these constraints are measured against the large areas of liberty young people now have, one suspects that only a society capable of ending virtually all coercion would satisfy them. Indeed, the vocabulary of repression constitutes strong evidence of youthful immunity to the forces of which they speak. The genuinely alienated individual does not know what ails him, and he certainly does not quote manuscripts of Karl Marx to diagnose his affliction. Nor are those truly thwarted in their "relationships" apt to wax existential or cite Kirkegaard to prove their point. These conversations really aim at characterizing the adult society that occasionally—but never successfully—threatens to envelop them: the world of work and marriage, of competition and careers. But most young people have yet to enter this universe or to face the choices that compromise character. Indeed, the attacks on the adult system are not so much onslaughts against an immediate danger as they are the reflections of unaffected observers.

But youth cannot be a permanent state. The years of suspended animation now last longer than in the past—stretching in some cases from pubescence through postgraduate study—but even this interlude must end. The moment arrives when neither fathers nor fellowships can be relied upon for assistance.

America offers her citizens no real option apart from entering the existing pattern of adult life. Few have the strength of will or purpose to stand in defiance of organized society. Many young people are content to live with minimal amenities for a prolonged period, but this is possible only so long as they remain single or at least avoid having children. When a young man marries and his first child becomes ready for school and he finds himself indentured to mortgages and installment payments and insurance policies—then he finds himself adapting to the regimens demanded for gainful employment and social respectability. (It is one thing to live in a cold-water flat when you are twenty-eight; it is quite another to send your six-year-old child off to the nearby ghetto school when you are thirty-two.) And as young people enter the work world, they gradually come around to defending more and more of the arrangements that make for domestic and social stability. Once embarked on this accommodation, most will conclude that youthful immunities are not appropriate to the routines of marriage and parenthood. And a few may even admit that their years of youthful experimentation did not supply them with precepts capable of surviving the exigencies of later life.

Yet, despite its transient status, youth will continue to unsettle the sensibilities of adult America. The feeling of no longer having authority over one's own offspring will inevitably demoralize a generation who once took it for granted that they were in charge. Whether the parents' reaction is one of dimly suppressed jealousy or vicarious approval, whether the avenue of expression is outraged condemnation or detached analysis, the most disturbing element will be the realization of having lost control. The liberated generation will range from adolescent rioters in the worst urban slums to advanced graduate students in the nation's best universities. From some will come protests carrying a sharp ideological edge; for others the mode will be aimless violence; and for some the outlet will be personal abdication or sensual indulgence. What all will have in common is their escape from adult example and parental influence.

That today's young people will in time graduate from the years of experimentation should not be allowed to obscure the fact that society will keep providing new entrants. The forty million people now between the ages of fourteen and twenty-eight will soon be succeeded by their younger brothers and sisters—indeed, by offspring of their own. To hope for a return to an era of obedient children, of docile adolescents, is naïve. To assume there will be a reversion to puritanical forbearance—that the "pendulum will swing in the other direction"—is to underestimate the impact of technological innovation on youthful spirits. Puritanism is possible in eras of scarcity or at the advent of revolutionary regimes: both these conditions seem unlikely in the American future.

In exempting its sons and daughters from inhibitions and obligations, American society has created a generation both able and anxious to tell its elders some uncomfortable truths about the character and quality of their own and the nation's life. Yet Americans have always been bothered by disunity: hence the stress on agreement and continuity, and the insistence that our classes do not struggle. But the barricades between the generations have been raised just at a time when racial and economic tensions are also heightening. Adults are concerned, but show little inclination or ability to understand those who question established institutions. This incomprehension will continue even when the uneasy parents are individuals who themselves passed judgment on adult authority in their own youth. A parent who crosses the age of thirty becomes a different person. His character and outlook are transformed by the demands of the productive world: he thus looks on his children not as creatures in whose sandals he once stood, but rather as an enemy encampment, citizens of a realm of freedom which adult Americans can never regain.

10: Democracy and the Scholarly Calling

THE ACCUMULATION of knowledge is one of the fastest-growing fields of employment in American life. More people than ever before now earn respectable livings by producing and interpreting information about the world's physical, social, and aesthetic environment. And while this enterprise is conducted in a wide variety of settings—ranging from huge industrial laboratories to backwoods historical societies—the nation's colleges and universities continue to serve as the major repositories of basic research and serious scholarship.

My concern here is with the quality of the knowledge being produced by the American academic community; and my argument will be that the character of this knowledge is in large measure a function of the kind of people who bring it into being. Such a statement requires a few words on the new prominence of education in our national life. For while instruction and scholarship are often separate endeavors, the two are usually carried out by the same people, and a rise in research activity is closely related to the upsurge in student enrollments.

Postwar prosperity has, of course, greatly expanded higher education. Our affluent and increasingly automated society can afford to exempt most of its youthful population from the unpleasantness of productive labor, allowing them to extend their years in surroundings we call academic. Public and private institutions have been created or expanded to accommodate the new millions of American offspring intent on entering the middle class. Parents and children alike realize that the lack of an academic credential can mean a lifetime of social inferiority and economic inertia. Higher education thus becomes an escalator to new heights, a vehicle that permits one to pass fellow citizens who are otherwise his equals in talent and aptitudes.

Another, less commented-upon, consequence of the expansion of the educational enterprise concerns the adults hired for the ostensible purpose of teaching in colleges and universities.

The contemporary professor, in contrast to most of his predecessors, is expected to be a productive scholar. Certainly he is better paid, more generously equipped, and is released from instructional obligations to a far greater extent than ever before. This is so not only on the wealthy and prestigeful campuses; even second- and third-ranking colleges and universities encourage their faculties to do research that will enhance institutional reputations. Fewer and fewer of the nation's colleges give promotions simply on the basis of dedicated teaching. More and more at least go through the motions of requiring some tokens of published output. Not only, then, are there more professors than ever before, but a greater proportion of them spend more of their time in some form of scholarship.

This is plainly a move in a democratic direction. A society able to expand its middle-class occupations—faculty membership surely fits this category—automatically creates new opportunities for individuals who in other circumstances would have had a less prepossessing status. The number of salaried professors now approaches twenty times what it was at the turn of the century.* Faculty positions have been opened to many people who might previously have been denied entry. Not a few of these are able individuals whose inauspicious social origins would probably have unfairly disqualified them in less egalitarian generations.

But there is another side to this development. The statistics do *not* suggest that professors of a generation ago have been replaced by new academics who, due to the profession's more equitable standards of entry, exhibit greater intelligence and ability. They imply, on the contrary, a group that is now both quantitatively and qualitatively different from what existed before.

I am persuaded that the growth in academic employ-

---

* In 1900, 41 out of every 100,000 employed Americans were college or university professors. By 1964, more than 700 out of every 100,000 had faculty positions.

ment has had the inevitable effect of diluting the quality of the scholarly calling.* For every individual of superior intellect admitted to the academic fold in recent years, several newly created places have been filled by persons of mediocre capacities. The idea that any profession can undergo so great a numerical expansion and still maintain the quality it hitherto had is one of the major illusions of democracies. Such sophistry can, of course, raise the esteem of those recently admitted to professional standing. It is not the first time that reality has been redefined in order to encourage self-congratulation.

The democratic process is now a part of academe, and it is no longer possible to create a caste system wherein the elite are liberated for research while their underendowed colleagues are confined to teaching. The assumption that all professors are entitled to participate in the creation of new understanding cannot but have an effect on the character of the knowledge produced.

When individuals of average ability try to increase society's fund of information and understanding, they are soon led to recast prevailing conceptions of knowledge in ways that will make possible its accumulation by persons of limited talent. This process is endemic in a democracy, where individuals must persuade both themselves and others of their qualifications for once exclusive occupa-

---

* This is not, of course, to argue that all of the knowledge currently being produced fails to meet standards adhered to in previous generations. Any such assertion would be idiotic. Rather I am saying that, due to the relative and absolute growth in the number of scholars, most of the research performed today must be judged inferior when assessed by any reasonable criteria. (Let me add, quite hastily, that there is no possible way of measuring the quality of scholarship. All evaluations in this area are inevitably idiosyncratic.)

tions. (This, for example, is why "excellence" is found in so many ordinary achievements. Generous, even indiscriminate, distribution of commendation is one of the defense mechanisms of a democratic society.) But if the path of prudence is mutual congratulation, traditional notions of knowledge must be reconstituted so that more people can qualify to extend the scholarly frontiers—even if their intellects were probably intended for less demanding tasks.

I allude to the strategies fashioned by individuals determined to legitimate their presence in newly achieved positions. However, while an affluent democracy can expand career opportunities, it cannot so easily bestow on the new arrivals a sense of personal security and self-confidence. Even if his ascent has been relatively effortless, it is difficult for such a person to convince himself that he fully deserves his rewards. My concern, therefore, is with the insecurities that infect the scholarly community as well as democracy's less literate citizenry. Insecure people will always seek ways of justifying their status and enhancing their self-esteem.

The scholarly system, not surprisingly, adapts itself to the needs of its members. With so many careers at stake, a kind of collective security evolves, based on an agreement that lack of outstanding ability need not exclude an individual from gaining a respectable reputation. The battle for survival must by no means be a war of all against all. On the contrary, ententes can be formed wherein all members are protected from unfair competition by pegging expectations of intellectual achievement at a reasonable level. Let me illustrate how inadequacies are concealed.

Contemporary research tends to turn to areas and methods of study where the scholar, no matter what he does, will never be confronted with the accusation that he is wrong. Academic knowledge has ceased to be a broad-gauged pursuit of truth and has become instead the accumulation of correct information and interpretations. The lifetime output of a modern scholar can, therefore, consist of quite reputable findings, not a single one of which is liable to attack on the ground that it is in error. To recast the contours of knowledge so that those engaged in its creation are invariably right is not an endeavor demanding omniscience or infallibility. One only needs to focus on questions where research will yield unexceptionable results, and to eschew topics that might give rise to false reasoning. (I hope it is not necessary to point out that I am not opposed to the production of truth, nor am I proposing the extension or expansion of error. I am simply suggesting that when scholarship is combined with insecure status, its participants will be reluctant to venture into territory that may turn out to be personally threatening.)

Mediocre minds work best when rules are explicit and everyone in an enterprise follows settled procedures. This is how we characterize that phenomenon called the bureaucratic mentality, and I will only add that many of those now in the scholarly calling would have been clerks in a less mobile era. Minimizing individual discretion in the accumulation and analysis of information ensures that individuals of ordinary capacity will be able to produce professionally acceptable findings. Indeed, the whole concept of "replicable" research assumes that an original mind is neither wanted nor needed: for when the rules are followed, another scholar can go through the same or similar motions and emerge with parallel conclusions. Thus the great care taken to establish the impeccability of research procedures. Few scholars can afford to stand their ground with the eccentric assertion, "This is the way reality appears to me." Rather, pains are taken to exorcise personality from perception, and the message becomes, "This is reality when viewed through the lens of this method." If the methodology is professionally acceptable, as it usually is, then the elements of reality it reveals are usually quite commonplace. Thus the devotion of scholars of varied disciplines to what they call "the data"—items of information gathered by agreed-upon research methods. So long as a scholar is assiduous enough to "stick to the data" and is sufficiently self-disciplined to omit his personal impressions, there is little risk that his conclusions will be faulted on any but technical grounds. (I suppose I must once more profess that I harbor no ingrained objection to the "scientific method" as such. My unease stems from its over-application in scholarly study and, more important, from the truncation of accredited knowledge into only those facets of reality that may be uncovered by established methodological precepts.)

With an increasing quota of scholars professing detachment and disinterest, it is worth asking why so many are attracted to this particular stance. Objectivity is not the only possible posture: indeed, academics of earlier eras devoted themselves to elaborating their own philosophies and beliefs. But to adumbrate one's own conception of the Good or the Beautiful is to risk attack from

several quarters. There will be, first, the onslaught of
those committed to opposed persuasions; more critical,
there will be the reactions of professional colleagues inclined to dismiss the scholar who indulges in the dilation
of his own preferences. A safety is to be gained by
donning the mantle of neutral coloration, for a presumed
dedication to bias-free research exempts the scholar from
accusations of unprofessional deportment. At the same
time, self-preservation depends on mutual adherence to
another ground-rule: that scholars refrain from searching
for ideological assumptions implicit in one another's research undertakings. All are vulnerable on this score, but
so long as one's findings are not egregious violations of
common sense or over-severe in their implications for
prevailing institutions, colleagues will refrain from scru-
tinizing the underlying premises.

Team research can always be justified, quite plausibly,
by the complexity of the subject matter and the man-
hours of labor needed for its successful completion. Yet
combined operations and authorship, wherein ideas and
information are credited to the group endeavor, are also
convenient means of masking the unimpressive aptitudes
of the participants. While one person of unusual ambition or ability may superintend the consortium, its utility
is that it provides reputable berths for others with lesser
endowments. The prevalence of multi-member projects
shows clearly how many of the nation's scholars have
discovered that pooling their capacities will yield a personal dividend substantially greater than if each had
exposed the limits of his competence in not-so-splendid
isolation. What I am suggesting is that when Smith enlists

Jones and Brown and Thompson in a collaborative venture, the last three end up looking much better than if they had attempted to work individually. (Smith gladly carries these satellites. It is, first of all, known as "his" project; and, second, the contributions of his colleagues expand the scope—if not the depth—of the venture.)

Closely related is the timely intrusion of advanced equipment into scholarly circles. Less and less knowledge now emanates from ransacking library stacks or isolated reflection. Research is conducted in the laboratories or out in the field and is then processed by the newest technological inventions. Tape-recorders and computers, jet travel and electric typewriters are accepted instruments of knowledge production. Not only does this elaborate machinery aid scholarly pursuits in a growing number of disciplines, but it provides mechanisms whereby creditable research can be produced in suitably visible quantities. Using equipment is a way of imparting a material substructure to one's methodology; the machine actually materializes the method. Reportage is permitted to pass as research if it is recounted in the appropriate style. There are, of course, common-sense limits—one cannot simply publish print-out—but equipment-generated information provides such a plenitude of admissible data that the scholar can fill several articles or chapters with permuted and combined elaborations. Here too the professional community is generous, with its members, allowing to all a bountiful ration of time and space within which to detail their machine-honed findings.* Whether the most

* Hence the so-called "knowledge explosion"—the sheer quantity of printed paper which makes it so difficult for scholars to keep up with

suitable image is of individuals hiding behind their equipment or simply standing on its shoulders, the fact remains that the new hardware helps to disguise the encinctures of the operators' intellect.

Perhaps the most revealing development within democratic scholarship has been the transmogrification of theory. Once a theory was an impressive intellectual adventure—not only a coherent arrangement of one man's observations but also a system of ideas inspired by his conviction and insight. I am speaking of an era when theories were few in number, brilliant in conception, and straightforwardly committed to a vision of nature, history, or beauty. Given these requisites, only one or two minds in an age would qualify for the stature of theorist. Lesser intellects were sufficiently respectful to disqualify themselves.

All this has changed. Deference ill becomes the democratic temper, and in consequence all feel entitled to wax theoretical. It has been necessary, however, to alter the concept of theory. No longer is a theory a congeries of grand generalizations—probably wrong, but brilliantly wrong. No longer, indeed, need a theorist commit himself courageously to a single-minded notion of history or human nature. For all their pretensions, scholars of a democracy are necessarily cautious and reluctant to appear foolish. Hence they hedge every generalization with so many nuances and qualifications that it runs small danger

---

their fields. But the real question is whether all this detailed information is actually necessary for the advancement of understanding. Very little of this new knowledge expands our insights or stimulates serious reinterpretation.

of being found wrong. Therefore, too, they include every conceivable variable or contributory factor lest someone judge them fools for omitting the obvious. Theory thus becomes at best a comprehensive summary or an exhaustive inventory, and at worst another lexicon of technical definitions and specialized constructions.

With such a relaxation of standards, virtually anyone can author a theory. All one needs is the outward appearance of abstract thought and the patience to write about the commonplace. The relevant ground-rule here is to refrain from pointing out that an accredited colleague is only elaborating the self-evident at unconscionable length. For in a setting where most possess only middling talents, no one can be sure that he himself is capable of generating anything more than exercises in the obvious. But virtually all of what passes for theory emerges as no more than convoluted syntactical exercises, even if highly diagrammatic and heavily reliant on symbolic notation. Certainly few, if any, of these attempts at high scholarship contribute to a significant illumination of worldly understanding. (Again, the mutual-protection system obliges scholars to aver that their thinking has been "stimulated" by one another's theoretical forays. These admissions, however, tell us more about the intellectual level of minds that need such awakening than they do about the intrinsic value of the theories.)

Because scholars, like other citizens of a democracy, estimate their qualities and capacities highly, anyone with the proper professional credentials is seen as entitled to confront tasks that were once reserved for a small circle of superior minds. There may be certain rude charm to these populist pretensions, but the ultimate output will be largely trivial or obvious and ultimately an anamorphosis of reality for the sake of enervated abstractions.

Given the personal insecurities infecting those who pursue the scholarly vocation in an open society, the ideology and institutions of professionalism take on an increasing importance. Professional membership allows an individual to sustain his identity and abilities by adhering to standards shared by others for much the same reason. The academic community provides such a haven; if the scholar conforms to its canons, he is girded by an armor he would lack were he to proceed according to criteria of his own devising. Such a membership allows a person to insulate his observations simply by asserting that they have been produced by methods that his peers consider scholarly.* These tactics become all the more necessary because there are, after all, some quite perceptive individuals outside the academic profession who are intellectually superior to the general run of salaried scholars. However, if professional rules of research are agreed on, then all who ignore them can safely be relegated to the status of amateurs.

Scholarly research has therefore become an esoteric, even occult, subcompartment of human knowledge. Because of the requirements that must be met, what can pass muster as academic understanding will constitute only a fraction of what man may reasonably claim to

---

* It is noteworthy that academics seldom criticize one another for the *over*complexity of their interpretations or explanations. Far, far better to make one's stand with a noncommittal multiple-causation, or even to err on the side of including superfluous variables, than to risk being considered obvious or simple-minded.

know about himself and the external world. Contemporary scholarship has become seriously alienated from the reality it purports to examine: it is published separately, discussed in removed surroundings, and defines its focuses in terms of its own choosing. Attempts to induce the academic professions to widen their ambits of interest are usually unsuccessful, largely because scholars know that their limitations would be painfully exposed if they faced subjects of inquiry for which their mentalities and methodologies are unsuited. And even when they appear to turn their attention to more significant questions, the results reveal that the issues have been eviscerated in order to make them fit the headings of research.* This is why an increasing number of individuals outside the academy have concluded that there is little in current scholarship to augment their intellectual understanding.

I certainly am not proposing that the number of scholars be reduced or that standards of entry to the scholarly community be raised. Neither of these steps is possible in view of the expansion of the democratic spirit. Nor is it possible to deflate the pretensions endemic in ordinary minds, or to persuade such individuals that yeoman labor in less demanding vineyards may be more in accord with their talents. I cheerfully admit that the burden of my remarks has been *ad hominem,* centering on the motivations of scholars rather than on the substance of

* Let me also suggest that what we call a "liberal arts" education is chiefly the transmission of academic knowledge, and on the professors' own terms. What professors teach undergraduates is primarily knowledge that other professors have created. Insights originating from non-academic sources are likely to be considered inappropriate for college classrooms.

206

their production. I have at no time suggested that the knowledge scholars have created is either false or invalid; indeed, one of my chief conclusions is that most of what they say is all too true. My intention, rather, has been to focus on the fact that not only do human beings create knowledge but that the shape of this knowledge will reflect the abilities of its creators. And in light of the expanded academic population, much of contemporary scholarship may best be viewed as environmental adaptations devised to provide honorable occupations for Americans of middling intelligence.

11 : Time of Decline

PERHAPS THE MOST beguiling thesis of postwar historians has been that our lack of a feudal past exempted Americans from constraints known by nations burdened with more inhibiting traditions. While this hypothesis is fundamentally correct, its basic validity has deflected attention from other facets of the American experience. Thus, while the United States never carried a feudal legacy, and no coherent class structure ever embraced the entire country, the fact is that until the Second World War most of the American people lived under systems of social and moral controls which served as effective instruments for shaping character and governing behavior.

In the ethnic enclaves of large cities no less than the villages of New England, in the rural backwaters of the Deep South as well as the middle-class neighborhoods of Midwestern towns, authority was acknowledged and re-

208

spect was accorded to those in presiding positions. Parents, teachers, priests, and pastors were influential figures, while church and school taught rules of comportment reinforcing parental authority. Whether in the Polish slum of a Pennsylvania milltown or the white frame homes of clerks and cashiers, Americans understood their place in the local community and the scope of appropriate behavior.

There was no national church, and no landed aristocracy dominated the social structure. Classes were never clearly demarcated, and government bore few of the customs or ceremonies which lend mystery to the arts of state. Yet the majority of Americans spent their lives in circumscribed settings which, if not literally feudal, nonetheless enforced regimens that tolerated little deviation from established local standards.

Prosperous landowners were accorded deference in most rural areas, and in the cities successful businessmen had prestige and power. Bankers, lawyers, and merchants may have been esteemed more for their worldly attainments than for their parentage; but if they were a governing class, they governed with no small measure of popular acquiescence.* Habitual deference is the psychological foundation of the feudal condition; and so long as

---

* Too much can be made of the "town meeting" tradition, with its idyllized portrayal of yeoman citizenries governing themselves amid Jeffersonian deliberations. In fact most of rural and small-town America was—and much of it still is—effectively governed by the local business class. By the same token, the typical city boss was apt to be a successful businessman whose wealth derived from his neighborhood base of operations. If he distributed loaves and fishes at periodic intervals, this was in large measure possible because his personal bank balance was ample for such generosity.

209

that consciousness pervades a population, the society will remain relatively stable.

In many ways, puritanism was the American equivalent of the feudal mentality. Certainly its strictures of hard work and deferred gratification tended to minimize social mischief. More important, the puritan metaphysic ensured that the unsuccessful would blame their own inadequacies, thus remaining quiescent as authority gravitated to their putative betters. Nor was this simply a New England or Protestant phenomenon. Catholic and Jewish immigrants also embraced this outlook, as did the poor whites and the even poorer blacks of the South. The great majority of Irish, Italians, Germans, and Jews acknowledged their proper stations and remained remarkably docile until they had ascended to more prepossessing locations in life—which many, of course, never did.

Again, too much significance can be assigned to the immigrants' "take-over" of city governments. Only a few rose to positions of real power, and only a minority were able to line their pockets through public service. The majority of recent arrivals remained unobtrusive: indeed, even the Irish who rioted against the draft and the Jews who struck against the sweatshops never challenged the bases of economic power or social preferment.

The condition I am describing can be illustrated by two of the controls that guided behavior. These were the dispositions toward patriotism and piety—qualities that called for submission to authority and a willingness to accept explanations provided by others.

Patriotic sentiment in America has never been roused

by sheer affection for our government, for that complex of institutions was always regarded with suspicion. Emotional attachments were directed, rather, to the greater society and the style of life it afforded its inhabitants. If Americans volunteered for service in the Civil War and World War I, an even larger number were prepared to accept conscription as their civic obligation. Citizens loved their country and were willing to say so without embarrassment. The point was not simply that young men signed up for service in time of peril. More important, the general citizenry, whether of old stock or recent arrival, defined no small part of their personal identities in terms of their country's moral mission. America was unselfish and unaggressive, a purer place than alien lands and superior to them. To be part of such a nation confirmed one's own purity and superiority; patriotism and self-esteem conjoined in unblushing affirmation.

Many Americans still feel this way. This is especially true of the working- and lower-middle classes, whose members are still grateful for the bounties of being an American. But for a growing number, to be more than politely patriotic is simply out of character. Reciting the Pledge of Allegiance or rising for the National Anthem is no longer an emotion-laden act; and a citizen's expressions of loyalty are increasingly based on calculations of how he will himself be affected by assuming one posture or another. Displays of patriotism are more and more considered to be juvenile, and fewer expressions of national pride are seen as sacred. This incapacity to straighten one's shoulders or shed a tear is, of course, a sign of sophistication and presumably ought to be welcomed. But the emergence of skepticism has weakened the frame of mind on which the power and survival of a nation depend.

Religion is an even more impressive vehicle of social control, designed to guide behavior by forbidding acts and ideas deemed injurious or immoral. Such constraints are best enforced by the communicant himself when he adopts and internalizes the churchly code. The authority of priests or pastors, the influence of one's fellow sectarians, and a corpus of precept and doctrine must all be in evidence if moral regulation is to be effectively maintained. And equally necessary is the community's ability to exorcise competitive tenets and visible temptations. Most Americans in the past were bound by religious rules sufficiently to ensure a measure of social order. America was not immune from violence and crime, or alcoholic excess and sexual impropriety, but there might have been a great deal more obstreperousness in the slums and small towns and countryside had it not been for the role of religion. Despite the virulence of Hell's Kitchen, frontier settlements, and Southern lynch mobs, the nation as a whole did not seem obsessed with threats to personal safety and security. Indeed, most citizens wished to be thought respectable and law-abiding, and much of this impetus was religious in inspiration.

Just as many Americans can no longer rouse their patriotic impulses, so a growing number find adherence to religion increasingly difficult. There is reason to believe that most people would like to embrace some kind of religious outlook or observance, but they have ceased being persons of the sort for whom religions are fashioned.

212

More and more Americans have reached the stage where they have too much knowledge about themselves and the world to accept either traditional doctrine or pastoral authority. A population exposed to even a modicum of modern education will be ill at ease with antediluvian texts and teachings; and as individuals grow surer of themselves, they are less willing to ascribe unusual qualities to fellow mortals who happen to be garbed in priestly vestments.

Religious identifications have not, however, been discarded; nor has there been a widespread renunciation of beliefs in the supernatural. Instead, debates and discussions have been mounted to aid the discovery of a new religious posture intended to be "relevant" to the needs of the day and to the sensibilities of contemporary man. Hence the spectacle of numberless seminars wherein congregants are encouraged to speak their opinions and preferences on religious reform. Activity of this order may be socially fulfilling, even intellectually stimulating. But it is wishful thinking to believe that colloquia will produce agreement, or that opening canonical doors to experimentation will reveal a series of theologies suitable for contemporary personalities.

My point is that religion diluted by discussion soon ceases to be religion and becomes yet another seminar where all opinions are equal. The desire to be religious is a yearning for authoritative guidance and supernatural certainty. Moreover, individuals can wish for such assurances even if their minds and temperaments are no longer capable of uncritical belief. The need for meaning and certainty continues to be felt even in sophisticated circles. But continuing discussions will not change character. God is not "dead": He is alive wherever there are people with minds so constructed that to believe in Him is relatively effortless. What has expired is not the Deity, but rather the capability of people to submit to individuals and precepts once endowed with divine authority. They may have mixed feelings over their graduation to these uncertainties. But they are what they are; the peasant's serenity can no longer be theirs.

Education thus undermines the pre-conditions for patriotism and piety: people begin to question once self-evident truths concerning the mission of their nation, and religious verities become objects of debate. What I am also indicating is that Americans *talk* a great deal more—and in a common language—than was ever the case previously. These conversations, moreover, center on subjects once exempted from argument and examination. An atmosphere pervaded by conversation is bound to undermine agencies of control. Silence, particularly one that is self-imposed, implies acquiescence to symbols of existing authority.

Hardly an area of public or private life is now immune from scrutiny. Everyone feels entitled to interpret reality and hold his own opinions. No small effort is required to think of a topic that cannot now be discussed in print, seen on film, or aired on television. Fewer Americans are capable of being shocked or surprised: there is little they have not already heard, and they can easily anticipate what has not yet been said.

Most fascinating of conversational subjects is oneself. No longer so firmly entwined by the bonds of social citizenship and no longer so clearly attached to religious or local communities, individuals become preoccupied with questions of identity and the quality of their relationships with others. Liberated from identities imposed on them by outside authorities, freed from conventional controls, people realize that they are on their own as never before.

Feelings of anxiety, however, need not preclude sophisticated discussion. One can perceive one's own predicament with remarkable acuity, even if the condition so observed is a rootless and uneasy existence. If the upper reaches of sociological and psychoanalytic theory are still elite monopolies, a growing section of society has a fairly coherent understanding of the processes those disciplines seek to explain. Modern Americans, in fact, know more about themselves and their society than has any other population in mankind's history. Certainly the mass media devote extensive time and space to imparting at least a superficial understanding of our social condition. (Clearly there is an interest in—that is, a market for—this; otherwise, magazines and television would offer different fare.) Few Americans are oblivious to their roles as sociological phenomena: even putative outsiders such as the young, the black, and the poor are able to discourse on the forces that have made them what they are. Much, if not most, of the new concern with sex—especially among the young—is part of an effort at self-knowledge and understanding: a conscious attempt to establish a satisfying relationship with at least one other human being despite the depersonalizing pressures of the greater society.

Yet self-knowledge remains a passive rather than an active condition. Knowledge does not necessarily impart the power to control one's actions, or the ability to create a more satisfying style of life. Imagination, courage, and strength of character—scarce in any society—are not brought into being by formal schooling; nor is virtuosity in the conversational arts evidence of extraordinary talent.

All this deserves reiteration because the desuetude of old agencies of control has left individuals to devise such rules as they can to give direction to their lives. But it is foolish to expect that ordinary people can achieve for themselves a feat that for centuries has been accomplished only by institutions of established authority. Morality is meaningful only when its tenets are taught within a settled community. Individuals cannot be expected to invent codes of their own; nor can they continue to live by rules tailored for one milieu once they have transplanted themselves to new surroundings. The disappearance of self-contained communities and the disintegration of the norms they imposed produce not only uncertainty over standards but also eccentric experimentation.

Most graphic of all has been the application of fresh knowledge and conversational dexterity to the realm of newly discovered social problems. Americans know a great deal about the causes of violence and crime, poverty and prejudice, congestion and pollution. They are prepared to talk at inordinate length about protest, helplessness, and alienation. Indeed, people realize that leadership is needed, and a growing number are aware that

government is the only instrumentality capable of bringing about extensive social amelioration. What is lacking,
however, is any impetus to change accustomed behavior.

For all their pronouncements about meaningful leadership, Americans are no longer willing or able to be led.
For leadership—if it is to be more than a conversation-
piece—requires the exercise of power and the ability to
allocate the society's resources. If government is to govern, it must be able to tell people they must stop doing
things they are now doing; it must be able to curtail private activities and privileges so that society will be more
orderly. Leadership is meaningless unless citizens are prepared to follow: to sacrifice individual pleasures and
agree to redistributions in which they may be the losers.
To be a nation, in short, a society must have a citizenry
willing to surrender a substantial portion of its freedom
to public authority.*

* I need no reminding that such a surrender is the chief characteristic of despotism and dictatorship. And I am as aware as anyone—and
more aware than most—of the character and consequences of totali-
tarian rule. However, Americans have used the specter of such
tyrannies as an argument for avoiding even the most minimal of governmental direction. Thus, we define as cherished "freedoms" a whole
catalog of pleasures and privileges; and we regard official intrusions
into them as the onset of autocracy.

What I have in mind are not the rights of speech, thought, and discussion—which are actually quite easily abrogated by democratic governments—but rather such "liberties" as that of the landowner to build
whatever he pleases on his holdings, of the driver to navigate his
vehicle wherever he wishes, of the manufacturer to fabricate any
product he thinks he can induce consumers to buy. That these activities are construed as inalienable "rights" and beyond the purview
of legitimate governmental interference is simply an indication of how
easily Americans can be threatened by legislation they find it convenient to label tyrannical.

If some perspective were possible in this area, we would admit
that we could give up a great many of our self-styled freedoms and
still stand at a far remove from an authoritarian atmosphere.

Equally revealing is our readiness to ascribe the most impressive powers and potentialities to government. Hence the conservatives' anxiety over imminent oppression, and the liberals' conviction that social legislation can remedy the ills of our time. What remains unconsidered is the possibility that the governmental process—by which I mean not simply those who govern but also the attitude of the rest of us toward being governed—is incapable of doing anything significant about the causes of discontent. (Take, for example, the unhappy condition of the American family: disappearing fathers, unfulfilled wives, rebellious children. It is idle to suppose that laws or appropriations or agencies can improve this situation.) Government in America was neither designed nor intended to restructure the society or remold the character of its people. And now, as in the past, Americans have no intention of granting to officialdom the authority to undertake such ambitious enterprises.

The controls known by past generations of Americans have not been replaced by new ones. Augmented knowledge has not brought that sense of direction or certainty which most men and women seem to need, nor is there confidence in government as an instrument of innovation. If most people would prefer to live with values and authorities they could respect, this is a condition they cannot have. The very opportunities their age offers have served to transmute the American character, making impossible the securities and gratifications of earlier eras.

I have postponed until these closing pages the few remarks I want to make about America's international involvements. What interests me most is not the substance of United States foreign policy but rather our ability to pursue the goals we have chosen. I contend that our military and diplomatic postures are in large measure shaped by the internal developments outlined in my preceding chapters. Indeed, the frustrations that have marred so many of this country's overseas endeavors can be directly attributed to the mentality of postwar America.

It has become commonplace to point out that the United States has abandoned isolationism. The sheer magnitude of our international commitments testifies to our concern over the course of events in virtually every quadrant of the globe. We can distribute almost a million men throughout Asia, and garrison nearly as many on four other continents. We send tractors to Colombia, vaccines to Cambodia, and powdered milk to the Congo. We have invaded Lebanon, occupied the Dominican Republic, and attempted an overthrow in Cuba. A million American tourists descend each year on European capitals, and several hundred millions of dollars are remitted annually to Ireland, Italy, and Israel. Our military forays, our foreign aid, and our corporate investments unite to make us an international presence with as broad a gamut of interests as any empire has ever known.

However, this is not the entire story. In its actions America may now be internationalist; but in attitude, Americans remain an isolationist people. This country's citizens have never identified themselves with the international obligations to which successive governments have committed them. The great majority of Americans have had neither the taste nor the temperament for these undertakings. The chief consequence has been that our

219

efforts at military and political intervention have been carried out in a manner that can only be described as half-hearted. If the American presence is felt by other countries—as it surely is—it is also necessary to point out that Americans called upon to implement and support this display of power lack the mentality for the enterprises to which they find themselves committed.*

A nation determined to be an international power must have a sense of mission. Its citizens must feel that purpose inheres in their policies, that they have been called upon to transmit their ideals and institutions to the rest of the world. As the people of Rome believed that they were imparting Roman peace and Roman law to all Europe, so were Britons convinced that they were carrying Christianity and civilization to lesser breeds throughout the globe. Communist China sees as its historic role the transformation of an entire continent, and a similar impulse will motivate many new nations before this century is finished. In these cases, military might is strengthened by a people's conviction that their force of arms is an expression of high political principle. Of course, such a persuasion is often irrational; as often as not, such missionary zeal can serve as an excuse for invasion and exploitation. But the messianic spirit makes one man the equal of ten and serves to inspire those engaged in imperial adventures. It is this spirit which America lacks.

For most Americans can no longer believe that destiny commands them to carry capitalism, Christianity, or the

---

* American investments have, in contrast, been implemented with an ebullient spirit. This has been possible because no ideological dedication is required for the sale of soap or the establishment of an electronics subsidiary.

United States Constitution across the globe. Indeed, a
growing number are persuaded that the quality of life
now known in our nation is hardly an exemplary export
for other lands. The all-too-evident shortcomings of the
American democracy disqualify our system as an object
for emulation. There is a growing suspicion that the
American nation has lost its credentials as a teacher of
moral lessons; that our presence abroad is evidence only
of power, carrying no enlightenment in its wake.*

Another encumbrance—hardly new in our history—is
that we tend to regard all foreigners as inferior to ourselves. Try as we will, we cannot extinguish the suspicion
that other nations are morally decadent, politically unre-
liable, or simply subsisting at a lower stage of civilization.
Certainly few Americans care about what happens to the
actual people who live in places remote from—or even
close to—our own borders. Despite all our expressions of
anxiety over the "freedom" of the South Vietnamese vil-
lager, the hard truth is that his personal life and fate are
really of no interest to us. And if the inhabitants of Alba-
nia are in truth oppressed by their regime, it is difficult to
find Americans to muster compassion for them. Given
this conviction of our own superiority and the patronizing air we display toward those so unfortunate as to be
other than American, it is not surprising that what dis-

* Hence of course the question that preoccupied the late 1960s:
"Why are we in Vietnam?" Usually the stress was on the first word,
for people wanted to know how our expedition into Asia could be
justified. At least some citizens were also wondering why *we*—the
United States—were there, for a nation having no lessons to impart
is ill-suited for the imperial enterprise. And as we embark on other
Vietnams elsewhere in the world, a similar bewilderment will be
evidenced.

turbs us most about Communist take-overs is that they enhance Communist power by conscripting yet another population into the uniform of the enemy. In other words, our chief concern is that the Chinese, the East Germans, and the North Koreans augment Communist numbers, not that those human beings have been deprived of their liberty or happiness.

There is no need here to enlarge on Americans' incapacity to take seriously, let alone understand, the aspirations of other nations. Expressions of nationalism are regarded as premature or over-ambitious, and movements toward social reform are seen as endangering either our own interests or the world balance of power. Our geographic isolation, our internal homogeneity, and our conviction of moral superiority ill-equip us to comprehend what motivates people unlike ourselves.*

Thus the stages through which new nations move as they establish their identities invariably alarm us. We belabor one-party states, cult-like leaders, and coup-prone generals. We are stunned when property is expropriated, when white settlers are escorted to outgoing planes, and we cry out in horror at the summary justice that condemns local landlords to be strung from lamp-posts or shot in village squares. If these are the new politics of new nations, we shudder as uncomprehendingly over a world where civilization as we conceive it is no longer secure.

---

* This ignorance, I should add, cannot be ascribed to insufficient education: from kindergarten through graduate school, Americans are assiduously schooled in the diversity of mankind. Yet these exercises end up as studies in the folkways of inferior cultures. The ways of foreigners may be quaint, picturesque, even inherently interesting; but they are not to be taken seriously.

While the cultivation of alliances is a time-honored strategy of international politics, the United States has always insisted that its ententes are more than simply cold-blooded contracts for bases and troops. Rather we prefer to believe that we and our allies are equal partners in a common endeavor. Yet when these allies fail to accord us the deference or gratitude we consider our due, the American reaction is once again to remind ourselves that few nations can be counted trustworthy. Hence the impulse to do the job ourselves—which is, of course, another indication of our basic isolationism, even when we are deeply committed to international undertakings.

Most revealing of all is the obdurate unwillingness of Americans to undergo considerable sacrifices at home in order to support official positions abroad. Despite all the congratulations we have accorded ourselves for the generosity of our foreign aid, an American citizen contributes a smaller share of his income to such programs than do his counterparts in a dozen other countries. More important, our military ventures are never allowed to become so costly that they limit domestic consumption or attenuate civilian comforts. The point is not so much that our affluence enables us to send guns abroad and still butter our bread at home. Rather it is that we place a ceiling on military budgets to ensure that our civilians' standard of living will be maintained.

This was certainly the case in World War II, and it is the chief reason why our victory took us almost four years to achieve. The fact that we won the war—albeit after forty-six months of fighting—does not prove the success of our military management. Why, for example, did the United States not rout its enemies in a year and a half or, at most, two years? My question, let me add, does not refer to the time it took to develop our atomic weapons. The real point has to do with our less than total mobilization of human and industrial resources.

Furthermore, a high proportion of the money we consign to military enterprises is expended for non-combatant purposes and personnel. An American in uniform is still an American: his pay is higher, his wardrobe larger, his diet costlier, his recreational facilities more expensive than those of soldiers in any other of the world's armies. Hence, too, the high ratio of support personnel behind the lines. The suspicion is bound to arise that we can only win (if and when we do) when we greatly outnumber our enemy in manpower and machinery.

I will not attempt to judge the courage of America's military forces as compared with those of other nations. I leave it to more experienced observers to discover, for example, the degree to which Americans are willing to risk their lives in combat. There is some reason to believe that a soldier who is not afraid to die will achieve more in the field than three of his more wary colleagues. However, the American military man prefers a more prudent course. While "he who fights and runs away may live to fight another day" does not appear in our military handbooks, even the professionals who command our fighting forces find themselves having to adjust their strategy to their subordinates' love of life. (Anyway, Goldsmith's lines beg the question. Men who take risks are not invariably killed; very often the enemy is bluffing.) For the other side of the coin, it should be noted that the United States awards more medals per capita than most other nations; but even this, I fear, is not evidence of greater American valor. Every country, after all, sets its own standards of bravery.

Were Americans at home willing to live more aus-terely, this nation would have the wherewithal to under-write a most impressive military effort, even including the creature comforts we bestow on those in uniform. And if our fighting forces could dispense with some of their amenities and non-combatant contingents, the United States could well field an army sufficient in size and power to police the world. But austerity of this order is tolerable only when citizens are either fighting for survival or believe they are embarked on a mission of moral conquest. As neither of these has been the American experience in this century, that fragile condition we call "morale" has had to be sustained by material rewards rather than emotional commitments.

Certainly the Korean and Vietnamese wars have given evidence of young Americans' reluctance to offer them-selves for military duty. (Even in World War II only a third of our fifteen million servicemen and women en-tered as volunteers.) The major reason for this reluc-tance has been the comforts and pleasures of the non-military sphere. With a widened base of prosperity, more people now have more to lose by a sojourn away from college or career. If it is true that public support for our recent adventures in Asia has been less than universal, not the least reason has been the enjoyments and advance-ment available for those who could avoid the draft.*

* Indeed, it may be suggested that our overseas involvements grow

I offer no apologies for focusing on our record of support for military ventures, for it illustrates the basic temperament that affects all of our international undertakings, whether or not force of arms is involved. A willingness to sacrifice is no longer in the American character; and the conviction that this country's beliefs and institutions merit global diffusion is in decline. What was once a nation has become simply an agglomeration of self-concerned individuals; men and women who were once citizens are now merely residents of bounded terrain where birth happens to have placed them.

The remainder of this century will witness a world in turmoil. Revolution and subversion, insurrection and instability, will continue to unsettle American sensibilities. Our dignity will be increasingly affronted by arrogance from unaccustomed sources, and our patience will be strained by ingratitude and enmity from people who once accorded us deference and respect. It will be difficult to be an American on such a planet, especially if we persevere in believing that we have a responsibility to police its recurrent disorders.

A declining nation has two major options: to continue

---

increasingly unpopular in proportion as members of the middle class are conscripted into service. Had the offspring of America's more affluent households been drafted earlier, the odds are great that those hostilities would have been terminated much sooner. I do not assert that the views on Vietnam held by many young people are not moral in motivation. After all, those of draft age are as entitled to make ethical judgments as are citizens too old or infirm to fight. But the fact remains that only a minority of young Americans have been genuinely aroused over the immorality of the Vietnam intervention; the more common view has been that it was an ill-considered policy.

involving itself in overseas adventures or, alternatively, to end its era with some semblance of civility and grace.

The first course would simply carry on the policies of the postwar years, casting the United States as a power committed to superintending much of the world. Relying on our material wealth and modern weaponry, we can persuade ourselves that we have the ability to impose order in far-flung places of our choosing. Deluding ourselves to believe that we have the resources to carry out these commitments, we will try to use men and money and materials to compensate for our declining moral conviction.

Yet repeated failure to achieve our goals will give rise to frustration and resentment. And the danger is that we may abandon not only all efforts at negotiation and diplomacy, but also the policy of limited war. The impulse will arise to finish the job quickly and cleanly: to use our ultimate weapons to destroy, once and for all, the leading powers that have encouraged half the globe to hate and harass us. If we take this course, it will at least be an admission that the United States has no other means of international influence apart from its military power. The crucial question is how long the American people will tolerate the stalemates that invariably result from our foreign interventions. Our patience may prove less than durable, in which case a swift destruction of major portions of the world will become a more plausible alternative before this century is ended.

The other option is for Americans to acknowledge candidly that we are no longer capable of being a great power. A majority of us would have to admit that our nation is in a stage of moral enervation; that we have no more lessons to impart to others; that the way of life we have created has ceased to be a model for people beyond our borders. Most difficult of all, we would have to concede that we lack the will to carry out a worldwide mission of redemption and reform.

To proceed on this course would evidence an awareness that our nation has a history. Such a decision would at least be enlightened self-interest for a society whose members have abandoned the responsibilities of citizenship and think only of comforts and pleasures. This sort of abdication is by no means unprecedented: virtually every European nation has relinquished its role as a world power and is now content to attend to ordering its domestic arrangements. There is much to be said for being a Denmark or a Sweden, even a Great Britain or France or Italy. Whether Americans will have the good sense and good grace to follow these examples is highly doubtful. Such a country must have the ability to laugh at itself, to admit cheerfully that it is no longer the presence it once was. It must be able to stand by as other nations quarrel and contend, finding ways of conducting its own affairs despite the bellicosity of near and distant neighbors.* Such a posture would involve seeing and

---

* My conception of "isolationism" is primarily political in character: a forbearance from deploying our military might abroad. There need be no retrenchment of our overseas trade, our investments, even our assistance—so long as these are welcomed by other nations. I realize that foreign investments can be risky—indeed, to the point of being endangered by expropriation. However, businessmen of other countries do not wire home for gunboats if their foreign holdings are threatened, and there is no reason why American investors should expect armed intervention on their behalf.

hearing much that we did not like and granting that there was nothing much we could do about it.

The most obvious counter to a proposal of this order is to point out that once we announce our retirement, the Communists will proceed to take over the world. Not only will they invade or infiltrate scores of vulnerable nations, but the security of the United States itself will be jeopardized. Visions arise of Red divisions flowing down over Canada—like Sherwin-Williams paint—and eventually engulfing Montana and Minnesota.

My rejoinder is that I do not believe Communist intentions include an American invasion. I will say no more than this, if only because my personal judgment on this matter and the viewpoint of those who will disagree can both be supported by "evidence" from recorded statements or examples of actual Communist behavior. But I do have every expectation that revolutionary movements of one sort or another will come to power in many of the world's underdeveloped areas. What should the United States "do" to prevent or extirpate these eventualities?

Nothing.

Such a stance would at least be realistic. For the United States no longer has the will to be a great international power, just as it is no longer an ascending nation at home. We have arrived at a plateau in our history: the years of middle age and incipient decline. We are now at that turning-point ancient philosophers called *stasis*, a juncture at which it becomes pointless to call for rehabilitation or renewal. Such efforts would take a discipline we do not have, a spirit of sacrifice which has ceased to exist.

America's history as a nation has reached its end. The American people will of course survive; and the majority will continue to exist quite comfortably, at least in the confines of their private lives. But the ties that make them a society will grow more tenuous with each passing year. There will be undercurrents of tension and turmoil, and the only remaining option will be to learn to live with these disorders. For they are not problems that can be solved with the resources we are willing to make available. They are, rather, a condition we must endure.

No purpose is served by seeing this epoch as a moral tragedy. Such a time was bound to come, as it has or will for all nations. That our hour of decline has arrived without forewarning is understandable, for the American people have never developed a feeling for history. We have, on the contrary, been taught that ours would always be a saga of achievements moving ever upward and outward.

Yet despite our habitual optimism, there are signs that some Americans already sense the reality of their condition, even if they are unable to articulate its implications. This bewilderment is also understandable, if only because the American experience has never provided the vision or vocabulary to describe a time of decline. Here, too, we have been instructed that America was different, that what has happened to other nations could never happen to us. Nor can we bring ourselves to believe that our society's foundations may be disintegrating even while its outer surface bears the hallmarks of contentment and material prosperity.

The American people will continue to produce new

generations and carry on with the business of life to the best of their individual abilities. Abroad, they will either make peace with a world they cannot master, or they will turn it into a battleground for yet another century of war. Closer to home, however, Americans will learn to live with danger and discomfort, for this condition is the inevitable accompaniment of democracy in its declining years.

Acknowledgments

IN 1962 I WAS awarded a fellowship by the Ford Foundation
which enabled me to spend twelve months studying the character and contours of the American corporation. Some of
the conclusions arising out of that year's work are summar-
ized in Chapter Three of this book, several parts of which
have previously appeared in print. I wish to thank the publishers of *The New Sociology* (Oxford University Press),
The Corporation Take-Over (Harper & Row), and *The
New York Times Magazine* for their permission to reprint
this material.

I am doubly indebted to my friend and colleague Clinton
Rossiter for his comments while this book was in its final
stages, and also for providing me with a progression of intelligent and attractive secretaries. A similar debt is owed to
my father, Louis M. Hacker, for his painstaking review of
the manuscript; his suggestions came just when they were
most needed, accompanied by that generosity of spirit which

233

has characterized all of our relationships. Finally, an expression of appreciation to Robert Zenowich of Atheneum, whose encouragement and assistance went far beyond an editor's obligation to an author.

A. H.

Ithaca, New York
November 1969

Index

Adolescence, 188*n*
American Telephone and Telegraph Company, 53
Antitrust Division of Justice Department, 44
Authority
  community size and, 33
  parental, 181–84
  traditional, 5–6
  See also Social control

Bagehot, Walter, 63
Bell laboratories, 53
Birth control, 55–56
Blacks
  changing status of, 96–125
  liberalism and, 150–51
  migration of, 102–3
  new middle class and, 115–25

Blacks (*continued*)
  possible insurrection of, 110–111
  Southern economy and, 101–102
Bourgeoisie, 19–20
Bureaucracy, 17–22
  daily life of, 21
  rise in World War II of, 16–17
  temperament of, 20
Burghers, 32

Capitalism, corporate, 66–70
Childbearing, 176–77
  contraception and, 55–56
Citizenship
  corporate, 71–75
  individual self-interest and, 6, 8, 148–57

City slums, 22–23
  See also Ghetto life
Civil War, 211
Community
  authority and size of, 33
  disappearance of, 143–47
  of youth, 188–91
Computers, effects of, 54–55
Conscription, 190
  acceptance of, 211
  middle-class, 225–26n
Contraception, 55–56
Corporate capitalism, 66–70
Corporations, 38–76
  "constituency" of, 70–75
  creation of desires by, 46–47
  democratic theory and, 41–43
  education and, 47
  "elite" of, 59–66
  limits on, 44–45
  migration and, 48
  new middle class and, 48–51
  as social power, 40, 42–43
  stockholders in, 40–41
  technology and, 52–58

Day-care centers, 89n
Decline of America, *see* National decline
Democracy, 195–98
Democratic spirit, 4–5
Democratic theory, 41–43
Depression, the, 10, 12, 15
Discussion, spreading of, 214–215

Edsel, the (automobile), 51

Education
  corporations and, 47
  democracy and, 195–98
  effects of, 214
  "liberal arts," 206n
Elderly people, 84–86
Entrepreneurial strata, 19–20
Equality as attitude of prosperity, 9–10
Ethnic assimilation, 14
Executives, 59–66
  personality of, 62–63
  selection of, 63–66

Family, *see* Marriage; Women; Youth
Featherbedding, 18
Federal Trade Commission, 44
Feudal mentality, 208–10
  puritanism and, 210
Ford, Henry, 65n
Ford Motor Company, 51
Foreign policy, 218–25

G.I. Bill, 16
General Motors Corporation, 51
Generations, clashes between, 185–91
Geographic movement, 22–24
  See also Migration
Ghetto life, 103–7
Government
  antipathy to, 126–29
  demands upon, 136–38
  homeowners and, 138–39
  incapacity of, 126–39, 218
  size of, 131–33
  taxation by, 133–35

Grapes of Wrath, The (Steinbeck), 152*n*
"Guaranteed family income," 95

Hamilton, Alexander, 57
Historical determination of national decline, 7–8
Homeowners, government and, 138–39

Identity crisis, 168–72
Ideology
   liberal, 148–57
   socialist, 189, 190
Imperialism, 8
Individual self-interest, 6, 8, 148–57
Individuality as illusion, 158–172
Information, research as accumulation of, 199–200
Instruction, scholarship and, 195–98
Insurrection, possibility of, 110–11
Internal Revenue Service, 44
Isolationism
   continuing, 219–22
   new, 228–30

Korean War, 225

Labor unions, 44
   decline of, 75
Leadership, refusal of, 217
"Liberal arts" education, 206*n*
Liberalism
   blacks and, 150–51

Liberalism (*continued*)
   ideology of, 148–57
   taxation and, 154–55

Madison, James, 42
Marriage
   failure of institution of, 173–181
   laissez-faire in, 174–76
   new middle class, 180
   women's reaction to, 173–74, 176–81
   working class, 180
Marx, Karl, 57
"Mass society," 34
Mental illness, 87–88
Mental mediocrity, 199
Migration
   of blacks, 102–3
   corporations and, 48
   of new middle class, 32–33
   during World War II, 13, 14–15
Military expenditures, 224

National decline, 229–31
   historical determination of, 7–8
   imperialism and, 8
National Labor Relations Board, 44
Nationalism, distrust of, 222–23
New middle class, 28–37
   blacks and, 115–25
   as corporate citizens, 71–75
   corporations and, 48–51
   marriage in, 180
   national character of, 32
   property and, 34–36

New middle class (*continued*)
  status and, 31–32
  transiency of, 32–33
  working class and, 28–29
New York Stock Exchange, 41

Objectivity in scholarship,
    200–1
"Organization men," 49–50

Parental authority, decline of,
    181–84
Patriotism as means of social
    control, 210–12
"Permissiveness," 182–84
"Pluralism," 33–34
Post-affluent generation, 187
Professionalism in scholarship,
    205–6
Property, 34–36
Prosperity
  equality as attitude of, 9–10
  during World War II, 11–13
Puritanism
  feudal mentality and, 210
  influence of, 26–27

Religion
  breakdown of, 213–14
  as means of social control,
    212–13
Research
  as accumulation of informa-
    tion, 199–200
  as occult, 205–6
  team, 201–2

Savoy-Plaza Hotel (New York
    City), 51

Scholarship
  instruction and, 195–98
  objectivity in, 200–1
  professionalism in, 205–6
  quality of, 194–207
Scientific method, 200
Second World War, *see*
    World War II
Sexual values, 55–56
Small towns, 22–23
Social control
  patriotism as means of, 210–
    212
  religion as means of, 212–13
Socialist ideology, 189, 190
Southern economy, 101–2
Stasis, historical, 229
Status, new middle class and,
    31–32
Steinbeck, John, 152n
Stockholders, corporate, 40–41
Suburbs, 23–26
Surplus labor, 77–95

Taxation, 133–35, 138–39, 140n
  liberalism and, 154–55
Team research, 201–2
Technology
  corporations and, 52–58
  democratic spirit and, 4–5
Tocqueville, Alexis de, 42, 57
Theory, transmogrification of,
    203–4
Time, increasing tempo of, 7
Trade unions, *see* Labor unions
Traditional authority, break-
    down of, 5–6
Transistor, invention of, 53–54

U.S. Justice Department, Anti-
    trust Division of, 44
Utopians, 167

Value systems, suburbs and,
    23–26
Vietnam war, 221n
    unpopularity of, 8, 225, 226n

Welfare mothers, 88–91
White-collar class, *see* Bureau-
    cracy; New middle class
White-collar featherbedding, 8
Women
    childbearing and, 176–77
    reaction to marriage role by,
        173–74, 176–81
    on welfare, 88–91
    World War II and, 13
Working class
    marriage in, 180
    new middle class and, 28–29

World War I, 211
World War II, 10–17, 223–24,
    225
    blacks and, 13, 97–99
    ethnic assimilation during,
        14
    geographic movement dur-
        ing, 13, 14–15
    prosperity during, 11–13
    rise of bureaucracy during,
        16–17
    women and, 13

Yeoman democracy, 23
Youth
    "adolescence" and, 188n
    community of, 188–91
    confidence of, 185–88
    impermanence of, 191–93
    socialist ideology and, 189,
        190

Andrew Hacker

Andrew Hacker describes himself as "a native New Yorker
(born in Flatbush and raised on Morningside Heights),
but after a succession of diplomas (Amherst, Oxford, Princeton) I found myself living in Ithaca and teaching
at Cornell University. An indulgent wife and a charming
daughter, plus a fondness for movie-going, mystery stories,
and my own cooking, have helped me to survive fifteen
Upstate winters." Now a professor of Government at Cornell, Andrew Hacker is the author of four books and has
published numerous articles in *The New York Times Magazine, Commentary, Saturday Review,* and other periodicals.